Reasons not to move to the country

JUDY RUMBOLD

Reasons not to move to the country

One Woman's Calamitous Attempt to Live the Rural Dream

JUDY RUMBOLD

with illustrations by Siân Pattenden

✳ SHORT BOOKS

First published in 2006 by
Short Books
3A Exmouth House
Pine Streer, London EC1R 0JH

10 9 8 7 6 5 4 3 2 1

A CIP catalogue record for this book
is available from the British Library.

Illustrations copyright © Siân Pattenden 2006
Cover illustration: Siân Pattenden

ISBN 1-904977-74-X
(978-1-904977-74-2)

Printed in Great Britain by
William Clowes Ltd, Beccles, Suffolk

To Calabria Road, fondly remembered

It was all Brian's fault

A straight, simple no was my initial response. There was not the slightest chance that I would even think about leaving London for the countryside. I dug my heels in, and dug them in hard, making sure my husband knew that these were no pushover soft-soles; these were pointy, vertiginous, city heels capable of penetrating long and deep, heels that weren't about to be dislodged with persuasive talk about huge gardens, fresh air, and roses-round-the-door bucolic bliss.

And so his campaign to reverse the inexorable downward bore-holing of those heels began. He had recently started a new job outside London, which involved a three-hour daily round-trip to East Anglia. Each night, he returned home shattered, muttering darkly that he never saw me or the children, and complaining about the punishing traffic conditions he'd had to endure. A move to the country, he said, would fix all this, and more.

As I remember it, an elaborate show of sympathy from me was not forthcoming. I don't recall feeling even a hint of his pain. Indeed, I think I told him to get over himself and stop bleating. I wasn't going to abandon the work, friends and city I loved to go and live in the middle of a field. Why on earth would I want to swap the irresistible vibrancy of London, with its clatter and bustle, its addictive buzz and hum, for a dull, lonely life of bog-worship and pig husbandry? His new job on a stud farm had given him romantic ideas about getting back to nature and communing with the soil, but I was having none of it. Besides, extreme relocation was for other, braver, earthier people; people who had an affinity for country life, who grew up there, or had family links or friends living close by; people who knew their way round a pair of telescopic shears, could trot out words like trug and mulch without smirking, who knew their perennials from their bi-annuals, their oilcloth from their oily rags, and for whom such quintessentially rural lifeskills as jam-making, fishing, goat-rearing, drystone wall construction and septic-tank maintenance came as naturally as breathing. People, then, who already had identifiable traces of mud in their veins.

I had none in mine; they were gloriously mud-free. For

nearly four decades, they had functioned perfectly well on a toxic mixture of carbon monoxide deposits, belching factory emissions and burger fumes. They coursed with a singularly urban reduction of industrial waste, fetid shop doorway reek and nightclub fug. Smoke, stale beer, sweat and stinking chip fat – this is what powered my system, and I didn't want to change a thing.

I had, after all, only ever known urban life. Precincts and shopping centres, expressways and tower blocks, graffitied multi-stories and the traffic-choked road networks of Birmingham, then London; these were my experiences to date. I couldn't have been more of a townie if I'd had flashing neon signage plastered across my chest and concrete bollards for legs.

I loved the city, in all its gritty shittiness. The smell of heat and filth rising off hot pavements in the summer, the ceaseless din and racket of underground travel, the intoxicating anticipatory fug of perfume and promise that fills bars and restaurants after nightfall. I liked the fact that, in London, my children had friends from different backgrounds and nationalities in their classes at school. I looked forward, every day, to walking out of the quiet, leafy road where I lived and, minutes later, being absorbed into the chaos of street life. I loved the opportunities for seeing, at every turn, a never-ending stream of brisk, busy, interesting-looking people.

There were times, of course, when I joined in the dinner-party hand-wringing about the grime, the lack of space, the paucity of organic quinoa outlets and the appalling shortage of gullible East European teenagers you could exploit for cheap babysitting. But never in an especially heartfelt way. Never in a way that suggested for a minute that I intended to do anything other than stay put.

So my husband piped down and carried on commuting. But then he started bringing home, along with the tales of M25 hell and balled-up Welcome Break bags, great stacks of controversial literature. Glossy, thick-spined rural propaganda began to appear alongside *Time Out* and the *London Evening Standard*. Property sections from a string of East Anglian local newspapers detailing the outrageous affordability of chocolate-box dream homes with enormous gardens, thatched roofs and generous half-timbering. The sorts of places you could buy for roughly the same price as your desirably located but nevertheless poky London terrace, and still have cash to spare.

His habitual end of day moaning dried up and was replaced with upbeat talk about the unremitting fabulousness of the countryside. The space, the air, the great expanses of serene nothingness; here, you could breath without fear of ingesting anything health-compromisingly toxic. You could go all day without having your personal space invaded by a dragon-breathed fellow commuter during the rush-hour crush. And then there was the mile after mile of gobsmacking scenery he'd driven through before the depressing filth of London kicked in on the approach home. 'Like Tuscany, if you squint,' he said wistfully, after one especially entrancing journey through sun-dappled country lanes.

The night he returned full of vivid Italian imagery coincided with an experience I'd had that would guarantee me premium soap-box time at the next dinner-party whingeathon. My moment on the high street wasn't exactly epiphanic, but, when I got back home, it made me glance at a previously ignored copy of *Country Life* with something approaching mild interest. Pushing my youngest child down the road in a buggy that morning and stopping at a pelican crossing, I saw that his face – clean when we left the house but now smut-streaked and dirty from the traffic – was directly level with a queueful of belching lorry exhausts. He didn't turn his head away – this was a daily occurrence and he had, in all likelihood, become inured (and perhaps even addicted) to the fumey blast. However, that congestion-choked morning in Islington marked the moment when there was a detectable loosening of those dug-in heels, and I began to listen to my husband's rural eulogising with rather less simmering reluctance than before.

Bullish after his success in conjuring up Tuscan landscapes from unpromising Anglian fenland, he moved on to the National Trust. He recalled all those holidays we'd had in adorable stone cottages in the middle of nowhere. Remember the cosy inglenooks, the blazing log fires, the bracing walks? If we lived in the country, we could enjoy those kinds of pleasures all the time. I allowed myself a little dream. And what about the string of fabulous country house hotels we'd visited over the years, with their glorious libraries, towering four-posters, impressive statuary and beautiful grounds?

The dream wasn't looking so little anymore. Now it had layers, a plot-line, some sort of structure. There followed a couple of essential refresher trips to sprawling piles in Devon and Gloucestershire. There, we reacquainted ourselves with the stuffed, puffed-up and blowzily billowing magnificence of rural living given a luxury spin. Silver dinner cloches the size of heli-pads? Yes please. A dedicated pillow-butler? If I must. A trillion scatter-cushions per square-foot of sofa space? Bring them on.

I think it was while leafing through a personal welly-menu in preparation for a guided walk through adjacent woodland that the seed of a rural fantasy, built on 24-hour room service and round the clock slipper-valeting was officially sown. Living in the country, I could see now, would be one long leisurely waft around a garden laid with picnic blankets and croquet mallets. Day-to-day life would involve nothing more taxing than a little light dead-heading and an undemanding spin round a heaving greenhouse. Interaction with locals would be a rich and rewarding series of garden fêtes and afternoon teas, possibly involving traily white dresses and teetering stacks of delectable home-baking.

Armed with this intoxicating picture of a blissfully idle, lady-of-the-manor rural existence, I allowed myself to be persuaded to view a handful of country properties dotted around East Anglia. The estate agents' particulars, I had to admit, were alluring – all summer houses and stable blocks. But, peering over the top of my rose-tinted spectacles, the cottages themselves soon seemed to be less about sweeping driveways and imposing frontages than dingy hovels stuck at the end of remote dirt tracks, with crumbling brickwork and bleakly inhospitable interiors. These ever-more deflating weekends, lost up the byways of Suffolk in the days before Sat Nav, eventually served only to confirm what I had already suspected: my branches may have spread to embrace a little harmless daydreaming, but those urban roots remained deeply entrenched.

And then Brian showed up. Brian was a 'relocation agent' (read: countryside evangelist) who my husband had met 'by chance'. Brian was an omen, said my husband. He was fate come to call. He was salvation in a corduroy sports jacket. He was the happy co-incidence we needed to confirm that moving to the country was the right thing to do. To ignore this sign sent from – where? Hansel and Gretel's gingerbread cottage? The set of *Midsomer Murders*? – would be madness.

I had to concede that Brian was a lot less obnoxious than your average London estate agent, but still, unthreatening knitted tie or no unthreatening knitted tie, my position on the countryside remained unchanged. However, since he'd come all the way from Suffolk, the least I could do was send him away with a wholly unfulfillable wish-list of country cottage requirements and hope that would be the last we saw of him.

Quiet and secluded but not remote, I told him. Light and airy, but also cosy and homely. Big enough to entertain, but not so cavernous it scares the children. High ceilings, but with beams too. Massive garden, with a lake, its own chapel and a folly fashioned from the fossilised remains of eighteenth century woodland creatures. I relayed all this to Brian. We would, I felt sure, never see him or his expansive wardrobe of fawn leisurewear again.

While Brian was off looking for a house that surely didn't exist outside the imaginations of the creative team at Pixar, I found that, against my better judgment, I was beginning to soften towards the idea of a move to the country. Like home-churned butter melting in the warm afternoon sun of a flower-filled meadow at tea-time, my unyielding hard edges appeared to be collapsing inwards.

At dinner-party gatherings, I had always been a scoffer, and I don't mean of food. On the well-oiled discussion loop that always included schools, house prices and moves to the country, I was on the side of the rustic refuseniks, the sneery anti-ruralists. I was with the naysayers who believed that while the country was great for a brief, passionate weekend fling, it certainly wasn't long-term relationship material.

But now perhaps it could be: Brian reappeared. He had brought the full influence of his soft-weave charm to bear on the East Anglian housing market and found a drop-dead gorgeous old house in two and a half acres of beautiful garden (no chapel or folly but, as my husband said, he was an omen, not a miracle worker). And although I had absolutely no other reason to believe I would adapt well to country life – I suffer with chronic hay fever; horses make me wheeze; my sole claim to green-fingeredness was when I had a catastrophic slip-up with a liquid eyeshadow back in 1973 – this, even I could be persuaded to move for. This, surely, would adequately compensate for the sacrifices I would have to make. This would make up for the fact that there was no Harvey Nichols or decent curry house within a 100-mile radius. It would soften the blow of having to swap 24-hour buzz for unremitting silence. Even if we had failed to properly exploit easy access to theatres and galleries in London, it was nice to know they were there. Now, there would just be fields and mud instead. But this dream house was worth the trade-off. It had succeeded in yanking those stubborn heels out of their once-immovable dug-in position and had made me wonder, for the first time, whether or not wellies might be more practical.

But what about the rest of country life? Along with many other hopelessly naive prospective downsizers, I hadn't thought beyond the immediate dream of the fabulous home, and all the other kneejerk fantasies to do with self-sufficiency and barn-conversion, jam-making and chicken-rearing, cross-meadow rambling and blissful days spent running barefoot through wheatfields with dogs and children.

How would we fit in, for instance? Wouldn't it be a simple case of arriving brimful of good intentions, and being instant-ly welcomed into the village community? Surely we would shake things up in all the right ways. We would add spark to the local amateur dramatics society, bring urbane wit to the pub quiz. The qualities that served us so well in the city – grasping venality, insatiable acquisitiveness – would transform takings at the local garden fête. Anyway, how hard could it be? It's not as if there was a new language to learn. This was 80 minutes up the A12, not a trans-continental emigration.

As it turned out, we may as well have taken three different flights, a sea-plane and a four-day overground trek to the further reaches of the Kingdom of Tonga, such was the coun-tryside's foreignness. Which is about the point I realised that adapting to life in the sticks wasn't going to be quite as straightforward as I'd anticipated...

Reason 1: Mud

Just before we moved from London to the countryside, we had successfully reached that cherished landmark in any parent's life: the point where our children were sufficiently evolved to not daub fingerprints everywhere, dribble uncontrollably and spray breakfast at the walls. The point, moreover, where it seemed entirely reasonable to replace the dull, functional furniture of the poo and porridge years with pale rugs and a white sofa.

Two white sofas, actually. Sofas that were sleek, sexy and immaculate to behold, and which spoke of giant leaps forward in the journey to reclaim, from a child-centric netherworld of goo and primary-coloured plastic, some semblance of grown-up taste.

For the move, they were wrapped and swaddled with the care one might lavish on a premature baby. The removal men were given a long and involved lecture on their safe handling, and instructed to treat them as they would a collection of priceless china. There is, however, no truth in the anecdote my husband tells about me tearfully waving the sofas off like a mother bidding farewell to a young soldier destined for a war from which he is unlikely to return.

In the event, they completed the journey with their pristine upholstery intact. Once unloaded, with the men only slightly reluctant to use the surgical gloves I'd provided, they fitted into the house beautifully, adding a touch of sleek, contemporary minimalism to its crumbling rusticity.

And then came the mud. Lots of it. More mud than I'd ever seen before in my life. And not just straight, bog-standard mud either. Barely two days in the country taught me that there are as many varieties of mud as there are coffee permutations at Starbucks; thin, liquid mud; thick, deep, brown, viscous mud; mud like clay or, in best Starbucks tradition, mud with frothy scum on top.

Amidst all this diversity however, there was a stand-out, unifying factor: all varieties of mud left their mark. Upsetting, alarming, skiddy marks. Tread marks and footprints and gloopy spatter marks, some removeable, but most indelible. It took fewer than 72 hours of country living for our treasured sofas and rugs to get comprehensively trashed.

But didn't we have only ourselves to blame? We moved house in the middle of winter, when mud and rural living are as natural a pairing as bank holidays and torrential rain. In the winter, mud engulfs the countryside and insinuates itself into virtually every exterior activity, however inconsequential and unadventurous. What I mean is, you don't have to be tramping through fields and marshland to emerge with mud stains on your sleeves, your trouser legs or the hem of your coat. It can be a task as mundane and workaday as collecting the post, bringing in the milk or getting out of the car. To simply set foot outside your front door, then, is to opt for the involuntary re-decoration of your outer garments.

I have since learned from other incomers that winter is not, in fact, the worst time of year to move: it is the best. People who move to the country from the city are usually exceptionally keen to give the impression that they didn't arrive yesterday, or even the day, week or month before. There is shame in looking like a cliched incomer, with your wide eyes and your clean footwear, and so any helpful outward signs of rural acclimatisation are exceptionally important. Under cover of mud, people are less likely to be able to identify you as a shiny, groomed townie. Mud disguises the box-fresh newness of recently purchased wellies. Mud makes your car look less like the ridiculous, needlessly polluting vehicle of a show-off ex-urbanite, and more like the workhorse everyday off-roader that is the first requirement of the established country resident. And mud will help to age a trying-too-hard Barbour jacket, bringing it closer to the look of long-standing wardrobe fixture that its owner craves.

Mud, therefore, is a good thing. If you are willing to embrace it as an ally, not a vile, omnipresent mess, it offers instant disguise and promises swift acceptance into the rustic brotherhood. It communicates 'belonging' more effectively than any Young Farmer's lapel-pin or Countryside Alliance bumper sticker. The next best thing to mud under your nails is mud on your hub-caps and mud up your legs. Be wary, though, of applying a light but noticeable smear of mud on the face; this remains a hardcore statement of entrenched country living and shouldn't be undertaken lightly.

I tried very hard to embrace the notion of mud being my friend, but it didn't come easily. I raged against it for a long time, cursing its ubiquity, dreading its loathsome squelch, and spending a good many waking hours scrubbing and brushing and attempting to stem the constant flow of brown into the house by way of children, other people's dogs and, it seemed, simple force of will on the mud's part.

Eventually, it battered me into submission and broke my spirit. I hold up my hands as a once houseproud city-dweller who has been defeated by the relentless onward march of the unctuous brown stuff. I now reluctantly accept that pale, serene minimalism is no longer an option where interior design is concerned. White sofas were a brief glimpse into a world where nasty sludge didn't exist, but a brief glimpse is all it was. No more white, cream or even off-white and off-cream. Brown, yes. Sludgy mushroom tones, certainly. Oatmealy neutrals and forgiving marls, bring them on.

These colourways are, after all, tried and thoroughly tested. They disguise mud in much the same way as, a few years ago, they disguised the poo and the porridge. It seems that I have taken a step forward and a couple back. And, in the process, more than likely left tell-tale brown tracks on the floor behind me.

Reason 2: The leisurely pace

My first inkling that the pace of life in the country was going to be a lot slower than I first imagined was during my inaugural visit to the village shop. I needed a carton of milk, and I needed it fast so, crossing the road to go inside, I adopted the customary eyes-down, gruffly monosyllabic air of urgency that had served me so well for so long in London. There would be no conversation, no pleasantries, no mutually respectful face-time; just the bare minimum of curt interaction before the purchase was complete and I was on my way home again.

But, from the moment I stepped through the door and saw the long queue of villagers waiting to be served, I knew I couldn't have judged things more inaccurately. These people were in no hurry, idly chatting and exchanging views on the weather (cold for the time of year, if you're interested) and I reluctantly joined the snaking, shuffling line. Along with everyone else, I had no choice but to overhear the louder-than-average cross-counter chat. The woman at the front of the queue was halfway through a long anecdote in which the words composting bin, varicose veins and antique copper coal-scuttle came up repeatedly. There was no mention whatever of grocery items or shopping-list requirements until at least seven minutes into her monologue.

Take this long in an urban retail outlet, I thought, testily, and you'd spark a mini riot. Not only that, but the cashier would be fired for timewasting, with the store's customer/purchase/profit target ratios severely compromised.

Holding court was the shop's proprietor, who seemed in no rush to chivvy his customers along. My first instinct was to do what any impatient, time-poor, self-important townie would do in the circumstances: huff and puff, tap my watch a lot, mutter under my breath about ponderousness, ineptitude and the appalling decline in standards in contemporary retailing, and, perhaps, flounce out without buying anything.

But this reaction would have been all wrong. This was leisurely, sociable, old-style shopkeeping from around the early days of Mavis Riley, and I'd better start getting used to it.

In any case, what had I expected? Just a cursory glance

through the window would have told me that this was not a set-up geared towards efficiency, high turnover and progressive, customer-led marketing strategies. In his brown grocer's coat complete with gnarled pencil on a piece of string, the man behind the counter looked as if he'd only recently stopped peddling dried egg rations and shoving illicit meat packages under the counter to women in pinnies and tan nylons.

Here was a place whose plan for growth and expansion looked as if it had ground to a halt somewhere back in the 1930s. The lighting was dim, the floor ancient lino, the cabinetry and shelving a mish-mash of old haberdashers' units and what looked like only fitfully successful attempts at DIY.

The notion of self-service had clearly not arrived in this part of Suffolk; if you wanted anything, you had to ask for it. I learned pretty early on that jumped-up townie requests for hopelessly poncey things such as crystallised ginger and curry leaves were not going to make my integration into village life any easier (I asked for liquid glucose once. The look the proprietor gave me was similar to the one I might have elicited had I requested that he lick clean the mud-caked chassis of my 4x4).

Groceries would be brought through from 'out the back' and then wrapped laboriously in sheets of newspaper, their prices totted up in pencil on scraps of brown paper. There was no such thing as dashing in and grabbing a few items then exiting in a hurry without conversing. No: you stepped inside that shop, and you were in it for the long haul.

Right from the start, this enforced sociability and what I believed to be deliberately drawn-out service irritated the hell out of me, but I knew this was entirely the wrong reaction from a recent incomer who, by rights, should be working quite hard to ingratiate herself with the locals.

My more patient and tolerant husband urged me to regard this enforced de-celeration in a positive light. Of course it wasn't prehistoric and deliberately plodding, it was charming and quaint and exactly the way things should be in a sleepy rural village where the shop forms the central hub of community life. But I felt increasingly guilty for being so slow to adopt this new, more leisurely pace. I put it down to the fact that it was early days and the impatience and surliness of the city hadn't worked its way out of my system yet. Like testosterone leaving the blood-stream of a castrated dog, it would take a little time.

When, a few years after my arrival in the village, the shop's proprietors retired and the premises were bought, gutted and reborn as a spanking new Londis (with chip-and-pin and self-service), the entire village mourned. I, on the other hand, punched the air and danced a jig in the back garden. I never thought I'd be so pleased to see strip-lights and Ginsters pies.

Reason 3: Chintz

Not long after our move, my husband started to complain that, with every bit of newly acquired antique lace-edged linen or vintage rose-print tea towel I brought into the house, he could feel a little bit more testosterone drain from his body. He commented on the chronic emasculating effect of being made to accompany me to a pathologically girly local shop named Swags & Bows to pick out yet more beaded curtain tie-backs and Victorian embroidered window panels. He muttered darkly that being in our house was beginning to feel like living in an old lady's knicker drawer – and not in a good way.

But what seemed to irk him most was the knackered old stripped-pine table in the kitchen, bought at a local auction, and the pure revulsion he felt at the ancient seams of crumbs that were lodged in between the warped planks of the table top. What was the exact nature of the debris? It hardly bore thinking about: nail-clippings from before the industrial revolution? Ancient skin flakes from centuries-old farmworkers? It wasn't unusual to find him, at odd hours of the day, going at the scarred and pitted table top with a toothbrush or a pair of tweezers, attempting to extract the tightly packed crumbs from the grooves. But the antique fluff seemed immune to all attempts at dislodgement and removal. It was there to stay, as was my resolve to do vintage to the max, to take this gingham-floral country thing to its ultimate conclusion, whatever it took and however much alpha-male distress it provoked along the way.

What's wrong with new furniture? he would wail. What's wrong with shop-fresh goods that do not carry the scars of multi-usage spanning several hundred years? Modern, sharp-edged minimalism may have been fine in London, I replied curtly, but not here. This is the countryside, and with country decor there are different rules.

Even before we relocated from London, I made what now seems like a bizarre and lunatic pact with myself to disallow any item of interior decoration that was manufactured after 1950. Here, finally, was my chance to embrace chintz, to fill the place with adorable floral prints, as befits a sprawling country house and my imminent tranformation from brittle urbanite to soft-edged rural earth mother.

Now I would become an avid worshipper at the gauzy, cloth-draped altar of Cath Kidston. I would follow her floral ways, heed her vintage teaching, and have my true, shabby-chic self recognised through the faithful and devoted application of threadbare pink items and car-boot tat to every available surface.

Clutter – that's what country houses demand. They need distressed paint-effect shite and ancient stained curtains like babies need milk. They must be stuffed to the rafters with chairs salvaged from skips, broken fire grates from reclamation yards and barely functioning wooden things bought at huge expensive from companies with twee names like Scumble Goosie and Cabbages & Roses – outlets set up expressly to exploit the exquisite gullibility of the relocating townie.

You know you've reached the zenith of creative clutter-distribution when you find it's impossible to make a simple, short three-yard journey from point A to point B anywhere in the house. There must be stuff in the way, things to trip over, bump into and knock down at the very slightest glancing blow from a sleeve or wayward trouser leg. To encounter the poor unfortunate who is employed as a cleaner in a relocated townie's country house is to meet a woman whose spirit has been worn down and broken by the sheer volume of dust and opportunistic cobwebbery that settles and accumulates on all the junk.

And doing country isn't cheap. While you are indeed striving to achieve the effect of casual, worn-in abandon and neglectful-but-stylish chaos, it comes at a price.

Those flagstones cannot be just any old flagstones, they must be hewn from filthy Yorkshire stone, reclaimed, and then transported at great expense and inconvenience from a remote derelict medieval chapel somewhere up north. Those chandeliers must not be any old chandeliers. They must be exquisitely fragile coloured-glass examples salvaged from a wrecked and dilapidated dacha that has been in the family of Russian aristocrats for centuries.

The paint of choice for country decorators is Farrow & Ball, which, to cover a couple of rooms, costs roughly the same as it would for you and your family to bathe in asses' milk every day for the rest of your lives.

Indeed, there is almost certainly a shade of white that would exactly match this milk, because white, in all its incarnations, is big in country decor (as long, of course, as it's not actually white). Old White, Off White, New White, Strong White, String, Tallow and Bone are just the beginning; choosing from the white range alone is an ordeal which, if undertaken for any length of time, induces dizziness, nausea and other symptoms of chronic snow-blindness.

A few months into our move, I had been overtaken by a kind of madness driving what was now the indiscriminate accumulation of anything old, floral, clapped out or useless. I was uninterested in all modern advances in interior decoration unless it was edged in frilly braid, smelled of rose-petal room spray, or had the whiff of dead pensioner about it.

I became a sucker for every magazine that had anything to say – however inane, misguided and often plain sinister – on the subject of country interiors, and believe me, there are a great many titles exploiting the vast market for town dwellers keen to release and express their innermost rustic selves through the stylish distribution of scatter cushions and gingham-checked jampot covers.

But this deliciously pretty *Homes and Gardens* idyll didn't come together as painlessly as I thought it would. I began to realise that you tread a very fine line between achieving the effect of attractively cosy, careworn, faded femininity and the appearance of a decrepit care home that was last updated before the war. In truth, I didn't have what it took to make it work. I appear to be missing the gene that allows one to make wise judgments of style – is that battered old jug perfect for the kitchen table, with its adorable Fifties paint-effect and faded flowers, or is it an atrocious piece of tat that belongs out of sight in the back of a potting shed? Is that multi-coloured rag-rug a witty and ironic statement on the notion of thrift and parsimony when aligned with an expensively distressed Shaker kitchen – or does it just look a mess?

What is undoubtedly true is that you need a large volume of high-quality junk for it to look deliberate, and not like a horrible mistake prompted by inheriting the contents of some elderly relative's loft.

Now we have arrived at some sort of balance. My husband's testosterone levels appear to be back to normal and compromises have been made. But not with everything. The kitchen table and its rich mix of historic crumbs is still there. Doubly frustrating for him is that he knows that the best way to shield it from view is to cover it up, which entails embracing one of his other bêtes noires: in the form of a faded-to-perfection Cath Kidston tablecloth.

TOO MUCH SKY

Reason 4: The weather

Before I moved to the country, seasonal change meant one thing and one thing only. It had to do with hemlines, heel heights and the likelihood of spots or floral prints being fashionable for the coming month. What it categorically didn't prompt in me were wistful thoughts about trees and leaves, burgeoning seedlings, scudding cloudscapes and mind-rottingly dull stuff to do with weather.

But since moving to the country I have been forced to accept that seasonal change is, in fact, a very literal term describing the process of one period of the year seguing into the next, with a lot of accompanying weather, foliage action and alarming displays of sexual activity among wildlife. No clothes involved at all. Not even a scarf or other small accessory. Which, to someone who would habitually spend a great many daylight hours pondering shoe/bag/hat combinations, is more than a little devastating. Anyway, I have found that there is no ignoring these seasons and quietly getting back to my fashion predictions and vitally important sleeve-shape research. No. They are like especially needy children, demanding to be noticed, insinuating themselves into my every waking thought, and generally making annoying pests of themselves.

It makes me nostalgic for the city, where the turning of one season into the next is a virtual non-event. Nature is left to get on with it in its own, quiet, sullen way. Beneath a year-round shroud of uniform grey, passage from spring to summer, and from autumn to winter, occurs almost imperceptibly.

It's all very different here. If a city's approach to the weather is furtive and undemonstrative, the rural way of things is for the seasons to fanfare their every shift and nuance with an enormous amount of bluster, flamboyance and general chest-beating palaver.

In East Anglia, there is much talk of the region's covetably Big Skies. In urban landscapes, if you squint hard enough you might get a glimpse of blue every so often between the tower blocks that clamour for eye-space. Here, there are no such obstructions, the skies are indeed vast and, although the snide rural-basher in me maintains that bigging-up the Big Sky is a slightly desperate attempt to put a positive spin on the unattractively flat, bleak fenland for which some of the region is known, it certainly has its fans. For weather-lovers, season-watchers and neck-craners of every stripe, there can be no better natural canvas against which to observe the whims, snap decisions and meteorological idiosyncracies of the extrovert Suffolk elements.

Which is great if you are one of the people who move to the country in order to re-establish some sort of connection with nature, to commune with the environment and be ultra-aware of the minutiae of seasonal change.

But not so great if you are unwilling to let the weather and its funny, unpredictable and often downright eccentric ways dominate your entire life. Once the novelty has worn off, the novice weather-watcher might decide that now it's time to take rather less notice of what's going on outside and get on with other things.

Forget it. Think of any extreme weather you've experienced in the city, then multiply it four-fold. It's not just that it's more visible – those Big Skies again – I swear it's more vindictive too. It is especially demonstrative and insistent during the rural winters, which are longer, bleaker and more challenging than anything I'd been subjected to this side of pregnancy and series seven of *Big Brother*.

Last February, after a testing few months battling the harsh rural elements, and finding out what all that upsetting green rural protective wear is all about, I began to think Chicken Licken wasn't actually just a mad fool with early onset H5N1, but that he perhaps had a point with his sky-is-falling-in hysteria. Winter skies in the country are grey and oppressive; it's like living with a enormous leaden battleship permanently suspended precariously overhead.

The unpredictable rural weather makes planning for outdoor events especially stressful. Unlike the city, where the outdoors is nothing to write home about and life is largely conducted inside, everything that passes for fun in the countryside – fêtes, fairs, camping, car-boot sales, marquee-based parties – rely on a dry field. Rural dwellers covet dry fields the way city folk fantasise about empty car parks; they make life easier. Things run more smoothly.

But dry fields, fields that won't swallow up chairs and shoe-heels on impact, are as rare as hen's teeth, and occur about as often as a total lunar eclipse. With every bank holiday wash-out that turns cake stalls soggy and maypole ribbons limp and dripping, there is the usual resigned conclusion: 'Well, at least the farmers will be happy.' But sod the farmers. It's about as comforting a platitude as being told your granny's just snuffed it but at least the gravediggers will stay in work.

After six years of rural life, and knowing what I know now about the wild vagaries of Suffolk weather, you'd think only a deluded idiot would plan an elaborate garden party for late spring. But that's exactly what I did.

It was, shall we say, a fraught time. As early as the preceding January, I established an uneasy online relationship with a man from the Met Office, emailing him daily – sometimes hourly – with requests for long-range forecasts. He was patient and tolerant of my badgering, I'll give him that, but he refused – even with the offer of substantial bribes – to give me what I wanted: a definite promise that May 29th would be dry and sunny with a completely cloudless sky. I tried other weather websites (of which there are a great many), desperate to find a good forecast. In the absence of any concrete assurance (would it kill them to be unwaveringly positive once in a while, even if it means telling the odd lie, just to keep dampened rural spirits up?), I made a rash, not entirely frivolous, pact with myself that if it had the temerity and downright spitefulness to rain on the day of my party, I would leave the countryside for good. I would sell up and move somewhere more meteorologically consistent, such as the south of France.

A year later, I am still here in Suffolk. For the record, the weather on my big day just scraped through with a cloudy but dry result. Nothing special. Could, in my opinion, have tried a whole lot harder. It did just enough to keep me in the country, and not one iota more.

Now, after another exceptionally taxing winter, my

thoughts are, once again, straying to the balmy predictability of the Côte d'Azur. I am close to making another pact with myself and, to make the French dream a just a little more real, I aim to raise the stakes. This time, the outcome will rest on a sunny forecast for a projected mid-October barbecue. I look forward to hearing the Met Office's views on this one.

Reason 5: Going shopping

A broadsheet fashion editor can expect to receive roughly three categories of hate mail. The first has to do with the exploitation of women, and the habitual depiction of seemingly undernourished, semi-naked girls within the pages of what purports to be a serious newspaper. The second deals with the absurd notion of devoting valuable column inches to a subject as frivolous and ephemeral as frocks when there's global warming to consider/people are dying in famines/entire cities are being swallowed up by earthquakes.

The third and, in my experience as sometime fashion editor of the *Guardian*, by far the most vitriolic, is that which complains about the degree of London-centricity in terms of clothes stockists and outlets, and the assumption that beyond the M25, nobody is remotely interested in buying fashionable things to wear.

I am a little ashamed to say it now, but I recall that most of the letters I received along these lines were greeted with a derisory snort before being swiftly condemned to a file marked Sad Loon, along with the certifiable ramblings of green Biro-wielding perverts and radical feminists.

I say ashamed because, having moved to the country from London six years ago, I now classify myself as one of these disgruntled rural folk, and I know exactly how they feel.

But I also know that fashion editors aren't malicious dicta-tors intent on alienating those living outside a five-mile radius of Hoxton Square. Nor do they have us all down as welly-wearing sheep-shaggers in egg-stained knitwear. They simply know what I now know: outside major cities, there are precious few interesting, fashionable clothes to be found. And believe me, I've looked.

Let's just say that, after years of fruitless searching for a countryside equivalent of Brompton Cross in among the thatch and half-timbering, I have been forced to lower my sights somewhat. I never thought I'd find my pulse quickening at the sight of the Bury St Edmunds branch of Phase Eight – a place I always swore I would never step foot inside unless very heavily medicated – but it does now. I nearly wept when I found my first French Connection concession buried away in a mass of tweed and beige rainwear in a fusty small-town department store, and Debenhams, once a place I would hurry past on Oxford Street en route to somewhere more interesting, has become my Selfridges, my Harvey Nichols, my everything.

Beyond the high street, country towns are not lacking in small individual shops, it's just that this individuality is less about fabulous, boutiquey eclecticism than care-in-the-community craft hell. Once you've fought your way through the irksome dangly stuff – the wind-chimes and dream-catchers and crocheted monstrosities – the clothes tend towards a gormless, tie-dyed slant involving a lot of shells and boiled felt. Or there are dusty old Fifties shops called things like Sheila-Ann selling garish polyester shirtwaisters which, at the time of going to press, weren't presenting any sort of threat to Diane von Furstenberg's success with similar styles.

Generally, then, I despair. If the demographic and social profile of a region was compiled based on the kind of clothes stocked by its shops, you would have to surmise that East Anglia is largely populated by retired dog-breeders and surfers with, perhaps, a smattering of legal secretaries soaking up the middle-age range.

You might think that now would be a good time to bring up Johnnie Boden (who, incidentally, I want to slap, if only for those horrible men's brushed-cotton checked 'pull-ons') and that burgeoning list of other mail-order labels willing to help rescue the parched wardrobes of the country-bound. But I refuse to go down the catalogue route. Buying clothes by mail order is like eating caviar in pill form, or having internet sex. A large part of the pleasure associated with clothes buying has to do with personal selection, with touching and feeling and the rush that comes with trying things on in a shop. Not the same as being handed a plastic package by a not very attractive postman in a one-horse Suffolk village.

So I will plod on with shops, but it's a thankless task. Even if the name over the door looks promising, the customer in search of something faintly cutting edge is generally scuppered by the personal idiosyncracies of that store's owner. The out-of-town fashion buyer is someone I would like to meet, because she is one warped individual. I imagine she frequently congratulates herself on her spot-on insight into the sartorial limitations of the average country dweller. She has us down as timid, unadventurous shoppers for whom a barely detectable variation on a jumper neckline is quite enough fashion for one season, thank you. Entire trends pass unnoticed and ignored. She doesn't like florals, checks or floor-sweeping asymmetry (we bumpkins have trailing-in-mud issues) and thinks that any funny business with quirky detail is best left to those far more fashion-forward and experimental folk in the city.

Now I am exhausted, defeated, and, lately, sense in myself a serious waning of interest on the clothes front. How else to explain the fact that I have been rotating the same two pairs of jeans and three jumpers on a continuous loop for about eighteen months now? Significantly, out here there are no style police to monitor my downward spiral, no firm hand governing the widespread mis-use of quilted gilets and novelty knitwear featuring pictures of dogs and autumnal scenes, and certainly no-one fashion-conscious enough to know or care whether I am bang up to the minute, way ahead of my time or hopelessly locked in a 1980s timewarp.

It seems that I have begun the inevitable, inexorable downward slide into nasty, fleece-based rural-wear. I am almost certainly losing the battle against the malign forces of The Edinburgh Woollen Mill; any day now, I will wake up thinking colours such as rust and mustard are still alright, as opposed to devil-spawned hues that anyone with an iota of aesthetic judgment wrote off way back in 1973. Perhaps I should be worried, but instead I find I am relieved. Lack of choice is, like naked skydiving and shouting 'Arse!' in church, fantastically liberating.

Besides, us folk out here in the sticks find that with fashion duly dismissed as a confounded waste of time, we can turn our hands to sending other variations on Outraged of Suffolk hate mail to newspapers, such as – and my subscription to the *Independent* hangs in the balance over this one – why, when space is tight, Ipswich UGC cinema is routinely dropped from the entertainment listings. If I didn't know that such an inquiry would be destined straight for a file labelled Mad Yokel, I might actually send it.

POT OF
RUBBISH
HOMEMADE
JAM

HOMEGROWN
MAGGOTY
APPLES

Reason 6: Self-sufficiency

By the time we moved to the country, I had more than proved myself as an adequate parent-nurturer. I had raised two children, was equipped with a modest range of basic cooking skills, and my housework credentials were impeccable. In other words, I had been tried, tested and found to be well up to speed with the domestic requirements expected of the modern working woman.

Growing vegetables, then, would be a breeze, a picnic, a walk in the park. Toss a few seeds earthwards, and apart from the warm glow of satisfaction and reward this self-sufficiency would inspire, I would never have to give business to those nasty, grasping supermarkets again. It was not rocket science, and I was bullish about my capabilities. If that ringletted girl

Monty Don could make the seamless switch from running a jewelry company in London to coaxing root vegetables from unyielding country soil, then so could I.

And anyway, it wasn't as if I was a complete novice. In London, I had dabbled with a modest herb plot, but the combination of slugs, cats and a garden the size of a pillowcase conspired to scupper my efforts. In the end, I convinced myself that what finally killed off the already ailing basil was the noise of the crowd from Arsenal football ground. Bawling yobs can't possibly be conducive to the thriving of green things. Not like here. Here in the country, there was all the tranquility a burgeoning seedling could ever want or need.

The opportunities were as endless as the garden was vast. When we bought our house, we inherited land the size of a small principality, with a river running through it, an orchard and two vegetable plots. What excuse could we possibly offer for not getting the best from it?

In no time at all, then, I would feel in my hands the satisfying weight of a bean-laden trug. Before you could say pest-resistant poly-tunnel, I would be growing neatly regimented rows of organic vegetables – from the humdrum carrot to wildly obscure squashes and weird varieties of calabrese – which the children and I would harvest seasonally, almost certainly dressed in layers of tasteful knitwear and floaty floral pinnies in the manner of a blissed-out Boden family.

But quite early on, I began to realise that it wasn't as simple as sowing seeds and waiting for shoots to appear. There were all sorts of baffling, unforeseen hurdles to overcome before we even got to the planting stage.

Such was our astounding naivety when we bought the house, the upkeep of a garden this size hadn't even occurred to us. Its requirements and demands soon made themselves known. We came to regard weeds with the sort of rank hatred usually reserved for serial killers and genocidal dictators. Throw in blight, frost and more pests than you've seen this side of a corrective institution boundary fence, and we were in horticultural freefall.

Still we struggled on, desperate to instill a bit of green into fingers that seemed determined to remain stubbornly, townily pink.

A colossal mistake was to grow stuff that appeared impressive but which none of the family wanted to eat. Runner beans: fabulously accomplished-looking the way they meander up a bamboo cane, but with the texture of chewing tobacco. Courgettes: the first ten or so are lovely, but if you're idle like we are and forget to harvest them, you end up with marrows – vegetables that no-one born after 1960 or who isn't called Robert Carrier actually likes. Potatoes: initially fun – 'like digging up buried treasure' said our children – but after a while, ignored in favour of Playstation games and, indeed, almost any activity that didn't feature soil and trowels.

Looking back, it was the stuff we didn't have anything to do with – the stuff that had the sense to dodge being touched by the dead hand of inexperience – that thrived the best and was most productive. Cooking apples, for instance. I take my hat off to them. Independent, ingenious self-starters every one. Alan Sugar would be impressed. Still, as they cascaded abundantly from the trees, healthy and delicious, following their own schedule, it was difficult not to imagine they were mocking us: 'Look!' they teased, 'We've done this all on our own with absolutely no help whatsoever from you incompetent losers!'

And, while you can have a stab at taking the credit for producing a bumper Bramley crop, only an idiot from the city would be fooled (and don't think we didn't exploit this knowledge among the many idiots we call friends).

But, as we looked guiltily at another load of windfalls that were slowly rotting in front of our eyes, we learned from a neighbour that there was something you could do with apples to boost your status as a horny-handed crop-wizard among country people who already knew that apples grow themselves.

Chutney and jam-making scores untold numbers of

brownie points on the self-sufficiency scale. After competitive cake-baking, it's the only absolutely failsafe way of proving yourself a real woman among more old-fashioned rural circles who believe that producing a couple of kids is OK, but jam is better.

I duly bought a preserving pan. It was a magnificent thing, a veritable superbowl among cooking receptacles, roughly the diameter of the Millennium Stadium, and I resolved to put it to immediate use.

I was as good as my word. It has hardly been empty since it left the shelf of the hardware store. It has been used for, among other things, soaking muddy football socks, bathing next door's puppy, and tie-dying children's t-shirts for a school project. It has been an indispensible bedside presence during any number of tummy-bug episodes, and has made several appearances in a drum line-up during impromptu rainy afternoon kitchen orchestras. I would like to be able to say that I will soon be able to add a groaning shelf-full of jam and chutney to its roll-call of achievements, but I'm not making any promises.

Reason 7: Country pubs

It probably isn't right at the top of the priority list when choosing a house in the country, but if a vendor told speculative buyers that just beyond the back gate, after a picturesque stroll past a church, through two cornfields and some water meadows, you would arrive at an idyllically pretty village, home to the loveliest-looking pub imaginable, it might sway your judgment just a little bit.

It swayed ours. A deciding factor in buying our house was the existence of an irresistible cross-country amble leading from a gate at the end of the garden. In the weeks and months leading up to the move, we planned and re-planned all the fabulous car-free trips out we would have with visiting friends and family. It was, we judged from Ordnance Survey maps, that rare thing: a walk short enough to minimise the risk of tantrums from children and not so long that it might prompt, in the more elderly and decrepit, seizure, wheezing and possible death.

For those of us who occupied the middle ground between hysteria and expiry, it was just the right length to justify a carb-heavy blow-out at the other end – complete with treacle sponge and custard if we were prepared to break into a modest sweat on the way back.

So, just as soon as we had moved and settled in, we assembled a party to test out this expedition we had planned towards and talked about for so long. The walk was everything we'd hoped it would be – bracing, beautiful and punctuated by stunning views across the Suffolk countryside. It was when we got towards the end of our wintry trudge and were approaching the village that one of our visitors asked what the pub was like. We hadn't yet been to it (this was in the early days of relocation, remember, when we were naive, full of faith and blindly optimistic) but judging from the outside – hanging baskets, thatched roof, dimpled windows, it couldn't have been more chocolate-box cute if we had opened the door and a ton of hazelnut whirls had come tumbling out. In other words, it promised everything we'd been expecting of a lovely rural pub.

Things didn't begin well. We walked in and, true to the old cliché that has the buzzing barful of gnarled local men lapsing into stony silence when the townie ponces have the temerity to trespass on their patch, this is exactly what happened. Amusing when watching it happen to someone else; not so comfortable when you are the reason people's pint glasses have frozen mid-air between bar table and lips.

Then a request for some ice in my drink elicited a look that suggested I had just asked the barman to produce stem cells harvested from the bone marrow of a trio of recently hatched hoopoe birds.

It got worse; we were told to sit outside because muddy shoes weren't allowed (but not on houseproud grounds, surely – the place looked like it last saw the tickly end of a feather duster sometime during the last century). They steered us to an outdoor area with nasty plastic chairs, broken glasses, some mouldering parasols and unkempt flower beds. Needless to say, it didn't feel like we were in the middle of some of the most beautiful countryside in Britain; we could just as easily have been in a lay-by off the M40.

Still optimistic, if a little chilly, we sat and shivered while we waited for our food. We rallied ourselves with thoughts that the cooking would redeem the pub's disappointing first impression. The reason the people-management left some-thing to be desired was almost certainly attributable to the artistic temperament of a creative chef. Behind the rudeness and shambling ineptitude surely beat the soul of a culinary genius… and other such delusory guff.

It soon became clear that the money that had been lavished on the hanging baskets and lustrous thatch would have been better spent hiring decent kitchen staff. Or any kitchen staff at all.

When our 'home-cooked' food eventually arrived, it turned out to be home-cooked in the same sense a turkey twizzler is home-cooked. It had clearly enjoyed more hands-on contact with shelf-stackers at Asda than with any chef. The words 'local produce' were, at least, accurate: the hair I found in my chips looked like a distinctly fresh and recently harvested addition to my meal.

Since that grim day, things have not improved on the rural pub front. Which is tragic, because when people move to the country, they love the idea that village pubs are radically different from the noisy, noxious, sticky-carpeted dumps in town. They imagine warm welcoming establishments where everyone – villagers and visitors, young and old – can meet to bond over a pint, possibly while watching a cricket match on the adjoining green and enjoying the languorous pace and surroundings. For incomers embarking on the long, slow process of making new friends, where better to start than the local watering-hole?

Well, sorry to disappoint you: most village pubs are as cliquey as the front-row guest list at a Prada show. I have been to municipal rubbish tips and felt a warmer glow of generosity and acceptance. It's just not as simple as pitching up at the bar, slap bang in the middle of a group of locals, and, by virtue of your wide smile and slick, urbane repartee, expecting to be instantly embraced as one of the gang.

For a start, local people who have been drinking here for years are fiercely territorial, and have their regular seats and bar-propping spots. Muscle in on their patch of floor-space at your peril. In addition, they enjoy unspoken exclusive stewardship of their own special beer mats, pint glasses and ashtrays. Given half the chance, they would probably also like personalised coat pegs with their names in block capitals and a cute accompanying picture, such is the regressive, nursery-like cossetting with which many rural publicans indulge their regulars. But make no mistake, they don't like Johnny-come-lately townie twats encroaching on their territory. You will no more be accepted into the intensely close-knit bar-side brotherhood than you will be granted the freedom of the gates of Narnia.

Give it a few months of regular attendance, coupled with a willingness to forego jumped-up London girl-drinks in favour of Suffolk beer the colour and consistency of crude oil, and you might be in with half a chance of eliciting the odd grunted greeting, but don't expect miracles. And certainly don't expect to occupy your own bit of prime space bar-side until you've put in the hours hovering on the periphery, silently chewing pork-scratchings and keeping your counsel.

Some country pubs, of course, have noted the huge influx of townies and attempted to reel in customers with promises of 'fine dining'. But, along with bubonic plague, napalm gas and Jade Goody, was there ever a more deadly-sounding juxtaposition of words? Fine dining is a conceit that belongs with 'stunning vista', 'hot beverages' and 'all rooms ensuite' in the lexicon of overblown, faux-luxury hyperbole adopted by seaside B&Bs and tourist information handouts.

The marriage of provincial chef and competent cooking is rarely a happy one. In my experience, these people are wont to do unpalatable, barely legal things with vanilla pods and capers. They should be made to observe a six-mile exclusion zone around all herbs and spices, and are not to be trusted with locally sourced ingredients, which they habitually desecrate. I remember a particularly upsetting encounter with a lamb and raspberry risotto. And the day my husband ordered strawberries with balsamic ice-cream in a pub three villages away was the day he requested that the expression gastro-pub never be mentioned in his presence again.

A handful of decent places do exist, but they rarely pull off all the elements necessary to a happy dining experience; if the food is alright, the decor is so intolerable that your enjoyment is compromised. Or the ambience is great but the menu rubbish. A recently refurbished 'inn' (get over yourselves: this isn't the set of *Bleak House*) in the next village looked promising, until it revealed itself to be a disastrous nouvelle cuisine throwback with pretentious, over-fussed food and exorbitant prices.

Not so long ago, I gave the pub over the hill – its roadside blurb now boasting both 'fine cuisine' and 'gastro-pub' – one last chance, and paid going on eight quid for something described as 'fromage à pain with spiced onion marmalade and julienne of salad leaves with fresh fruit melange'. Or, roughly translated, a ploughman's.

It turned out to be sweaty, supermarket packet cheese with nasty cheap pickle, some brown-edged lettuce and one of those part-baked baguettes. Simpler even than a sandwich to put together, in that the putting-together part is left to the consumer.

It's not just that too many country pubs have had the charm siphoned out of them by big brewery companies who care more about profitability and homogenous brand identity than individual appeal and idiosyncrasy; it's the fact that there still persists a city-based conspiracy that beyond the M25, palates are simply not evolved enough to do justice to decent pub food. We straw-chewing, crust-gnawing yokels don't go in for fancy stuff like that. It is a commonly held belief that once you pass through the invisible barrier that separates town and country, you surrender not only your intellect, dress sense and powers of correct pronunciation, but any culinary discernment too.

Entrenched rural attitudes to pubs don't help either. There's a stubbornly held view that pubs are for drinkers and drinking, not anything so girl's blousey as food. Eating – and, up to a point, any sort of talking or conversation – infects the purity of the blessed pint and is tantamount to the violation of something sacred.

That, and the fact that most publicans round here appear to cultivate a look that suggests they have only recently been released back into the community as part of a serial offender's rehabilitation scheme, and are good at repelling passing trade, incomers and, indeed, anyone whose family hasn't been in the region for generations and has virtually put down roots in that spot there next to the bar, between the fag machine and a supporting beam featuring a horrible line-up of grubby horse-brasses.

And you thought the simple act of ambling into a quiet country pub to spend a leisurely hour nursing a pint was one of life's less complicated pleasures? Think again.

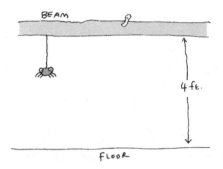

Reason 8: Exposed beams

In any other architectural circumstance, a horizontal wood-en structure erected in the home at a potentially gravely injurious eyebrow-height would be endlessly bothersome, causing pain, bad posture and torrents of profanities from inhabitants. If a builder suggested, as part of the infrastructure of a house, that a prominent low-slung protrusion right in the middle of a major domestic thoroughfare would be a practical, workable idea, you'd laugh in his face and show him the door.

Yet the rickety wooden beams that criss-cross through period cottages provoke no such scepticism. In the country, people seem happy to spend most of their lives bent double, ducking and weaving round houses built for midgets, just for the reward of living somewhere extremely old, dark and cobwebby, and which may or may not have Mrs Tiggywinkle and any number of mad-haired hobbity types shacked up in the inglenook.

Have you ever heard a bad word about an exposed beam? Beams inspire the same mawkish sentimentality as puppies and newborn infants. People go misty-eyed at the very mention of them. The thought process behind this blanket adulation seems almost sinister in its simplicity: beams are old, ergo beams are good (in ways that other old things – trousers, bread, people – categorically aren't). But I number myself in the section of society who measure five foot ten and above who don't necessarily think beams are unconditionally fabulous. Respect to the intricate and admirable craftsmanship of yore and all that, but where's the practicality? Before we found our house, we looked at a number of old Suffolk farmworkers' cottages, but these viewings weren't wholly successful. Let's just say the head injuries and shin damage accumulated during journeys up staircases and into box rooms and cellars designed with Michael Flatley in mind were many and livid.

Our previous experience of house ownership was limited solely to airy, high-ceilinged Victorian terraces, and this was like being catapulted into a whole new, scaled-down doll's-house world of twee miniaturism. The cottage owners had been careful to defer to the beams' imposing antiquity when filling the rooms. And I mean fill. Poky and cluttered doesn't even begin to describe some of the places we looked at. There was antique tat everywhere. Navigating these claustrophobic interiors was like being stuffed, against your better judgment, down a hellish warren of chintz-upholstered pot-holes.

Pretty soon, then, we instructed our relocation agent to strike beams off our list of requirements. Beams we could live without. We would concentrate our efforts instead on fulfilling some of our other kneejerk townie relocation criteria: roses round the door, leaded windows, a thatch so resplendent it could have been harvested from the luxuriant tonsure of Margaret herself.

So the fact that we now live, six years later, in a house with a great many exposed beams probably needs some explaining. All I can say is that we found that rare thing: a gorgeous country house with both beams and high ceilings. These beams would not compromise the basic human impulse to remain upright while standing; they would not impede movement or cause lasting cranial disfigurement.

Still, I have reservations. The beamed section of the house dates back to the 1400s, and my husband swears that there are spiders descended from medieval stock – in all likelihood wearing chain-mail and swilling ale from pewter tankards – living in the crevasses and dark corners of our ceilings.

And it's not just spiders who take one look at the intricate network of woodwork and insist on moving in immediately.

Woodworm, weevils and any number of eccentrically-named beetles put themselves forward as potential long-term tenants, before the man with the pest spray came in and indicated, in no uncertain terms, that they were no longer welcome.

You don't get this with polystyrene ceiling tiles, muttered my husband ominously, after a worrying incident involving a roof leak and a beam full of wet rot. More than once, we indulged fantasies featuring the clean, bright, nowhere-to-hide corners of the average boxy new-build. And, quite apart from any other reservations, beams don't look safe. I am thinking in particular of the one over my son's bed, which bows alarmingly – virtually skimming his cheek as he sleeps – in a way that suggests imminent collapse. That these beams have held firm for several hundred years should probably be cause for reassurance. But couldn't it also indicate that their time is now well and truly up?

Reason 9: Dog-walkers

Of all the solitary activities that can be undertaken in public without fear of disapproval, controversy or possible arrest, you'd think a quiet stroll in the countryside would be pretty high on the list. But you would be wrong.

Soon after we moved from London, I started completing a brisk daily circuit up the hill to the church and around a couple of fields. Like many people, I have tried and failed at all sorts of exercise and have finally arrived at the conclusion that the simple act of putting one foot in front of the other in a repetitive fashion is the only half-tolerable method of cardiovascular activity. Moreover, it is possible to do it without feeling the pressure to put Lycra pants on over your trousers, possess a working knowledge of contemporary running-shoe technology, or layer up tight vests in nasty pastel multiples. Best of all, walking can be undertaken alone, while ruminating on other, more interesting things that aren't to do with free radicals or body-fat monitoring.

But it wasn't long before I started to notice that my strolls weren't affording me the anonymity I'd anticipated. First, there was the odd sidelong look from a passing dog-walker, which I took to be the natural curiosity of a villager eyeing up a new-comer. Nothing odd about that. It's not as if there was any ostentatious thong-wear going on. I wasn't grunting or pant-ing or shouting 'feel the burn!' in an overly sweaty or obnox-ious way.

But then, as the days went on, these looks became more lingering and prolific. Now they weren't surreptitious, they were full-on and unequivocally suspicious. Why? In London, you could walk the length of Oxford Street in a soiled hospital gown, trailing your own vital organs and a semi-conscious pensioner from the next bed, and no-one would give you a second glance. But here, in an anorak, I was turning more than a few heads.

The fact that all the looks I was attracting were coming from people with dogs led me to deduce, finally, that it was the simple fact of my glaring solitariness that was alerting their suspicions.

There was no slobbery panting thing at my feet, and I

wasn't Janet Street-Porter, therefore I had no business being out walking on my own. Without a dog at my side, I was very obviously not out as part of a legitimate, twice-daily exercise routine, so exactly what in the name of Jack Russell did I think I was up to?

They continued to peer long and hard, doubtless in order to memorise the exact nuances of my facial features so that they might accurately relay them, when the time came, to a homicide detective down at the station.

To minimise the risk of my coming across as a deranged lunatic, a footpath-stalking psycho or a suicidal depressive in need of help, I could, of course, take the simple step of accessorising my walks with the kind of paraphernalia that would help deflect attention away from my flamboyant dog-lessness. A jauntily swinging decoy lead emerging from an anorak pocket, perhaps. An ostentatiously displayed polythene bag – the international signifier of the conscientious poo-scooper. And what was to stop me bellowing 'Rover!' into the middle distance, after some errant, though entirely fictitious, pet?

Then again, this whole pantomime could be easily avoided simply by acquiring a dog. In the countryside, everyone has one. Here, there is space in abundance, smells galore and hundreds of other dogs. Why haven't I got one yet? ask city friends, using the sort of aggressively accusatory tone that suggests I am a pathetic half-baked apology for a country convert.

My reluctance on the canine front has very little to do with the reasons people normally cite. I don't especially mind having my crotch rammed at some speed by the damp, hairy snout of a dog I hardly know. And being licked all over my face by a criminally halitotic animal who has come straight from nosing round another dog's bottom doesn't bother me much, either. I don't find dog poo half as upsetting as you'd expect, I am fairly relaxed about generous scatterings of wayward pet hair and I will happily sit through Crufts on a yearly basis.

What troubles me, then, isn't the animal itself, but the behaviour that would be expected of me as a dog owner. When out on my solo walks, attracting the usual sidelong glances from other, accompanied walkers, I have observed the way they operate and I have to profess total bafflement.

Where does it come from, the hysterical affability that dogs foster in their owners? How do they learn the sort of effortless camaraderie that allows relaxed interchange about bowel habits and worming medication within seconds of meeting? The fact is, I simply do not have it in me to be that sociable, that genial, that doggedly cheerful. Not on a daily basis. Not on a twice-daily basis. Not ever. I envisage a scenario at the rescue centre where they laugh in my face and tell me I am too miserable to be a dog owner. With my flawed social skills, creeping misanthropy and taste for the reclusive life, I would be a damaging influence, a negative role model. They would tell me to go away and come back when I've learned to shout 'Good dog!' like I really mean it.

But I fear I will never be able to utter those words with anything approaching conviction. If that's disconcerting for chirpy dog owners, too bad. If I emit the threatening air of someone who is about to slaughter the elderly woman in the remote farmhouse up the road, or, at the very least, bury a murder weapon in the bushes, then I am sorry. But not so sorry that I am about to adorn my solitary walks with anything more socially acceptable than a purposeful stride and a ruminative scowl.

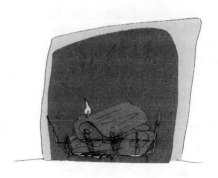

Reason 10: Log fires

If we were less than confident about our ability to take on some of the more exacting rural challenges, this was one we could surely tackle with our eyes closed. On a sliding scale of difficulty, with thatching and goat husbandry at the top, this was way down in the remedial category with manure-spreading and an ability to carry off novelty wellingtons with something like aplomb.

Log fires we could handle. How hard could it be? Making fire has evolved only very slightly from the days of cavemen and flint. It boils down to the simple business of assembling wood into something approximating a pile and putting a match to it. Result: dancing flames in a perfect ratio of red to orange, licking, in picturesque fashion, up the chimney. Pretty early on, the desire to burn stuff was urgent and primal. We'd suffered the dull efficiency of storage heaters and radiators for long enough; now it was time to allow ourselves the pleasure of squandering long afternoons prodding and poking with a set of pleasingly Dickensian-sounding fireside accessories such as scuttles and pokers and bellows. Marshmallow forks at the ready, we would finally know the bliss of gazing deep into the flames of a raging fire, dozing in the heat of its warming embers.

My husband had romantic visions of striding manfully to the woodpile and back, and then, with a grunt and a look of purposeful, furrow-browed propriety only previously demonstrated at family barbecues, coaxing flames from unyielding logs. But instead he found that there was endless fussing around with a whole range of fiddly combustible materials before he even got to the wood stage.

There was kindling, firelighters, coal and balled-up newspaper to consider, which, if you're going to get the best from your fire, need to be put together in a very specific order, like Airfix kits and Ikea shelves. One night, I ignored my husband's stern pronouncement that all firemaking duties should be left to him (subtext: it takes a man's hairy-chinned grasp of neanderthal survival skills to build a decent fire) and got a raging display of flames going in no time. But when he came into the room he shot a cursory look at it before flouncing out again, dismissing it as a 'girl-fire' and, therefore, somehow lacking validity as an effective heat source.

In more ways than one, a log fire tests your temper to the very outer limits of human endurance. Assuming you ever get the thing lit – there are all sorts of boring and prohibitive imponderables to do with, among other things, insufficient through-draught and an ability to 'draw' properly – fires require virtually constant hands-on care and attention, in the manner of newborn babies and risottos. Needy doesn't begin to describe them. You must prod and poke, feed and cajole. You must be constantly aware that a log fire is a malicious-minded entity with a very stringent agenda. Its raison d'être is to burn the house down or, at the very least, start some sort of dramatic thatch blaze that will bring convoys of fire engines hurtling noisily through your sleepy rural village.

Take your eye off that fire for one minute and it will utilise this window of lapsed vigilance to toast to a cinder whichever absent-minded granny happens to be dozing next to it at the time. Providing the round-the-clock medical care required by a terminally ill human is less stressful.

And don't get me started on chimneys, which need to be swept regularly if you hope to avoid incinerating the house. Will you be able to find a chimney sweep? Highly unlikely. Contrary to the Mary Poppins propaganda that has jolly smut-cheeked Cockney men all over the place queuing up to rod your sooty passage, the truth is, they are as rare as black cod in the ready-meal freezer at Iceland.

Don't ask me why, but there is a chronic shortage of people keen to do a job where you stick your head up inhospitably cold and dark places, accumulate lungfuls of soot and return home filthy every night. Consequently, the ones that do exist are insufferable primadonnas. Assuming you do finally track one down, you'll be lucky to get an appointment in the next six months. I've known shops selling new-season Chloe handbags have shorter waiting-lists.

When, eventually, I secured the services of a sweep, he arrived dressed, thrillingly, in head-to-toe black. This was for entirely practical purposes, of course, but it was entertaining to think of him having a secret agenda involving a little extra-curricular rural spy-work.

Not that he really cut it as a suave double agent. With his smutty face and shock of ginger hair dusted with soot, he looked like a decidedly second-division Milk Tray man after a punch-up and a night on the booze.

Oh, and a word of caution about big old country cottage chimneys generally. Just as stuff goes up them, stuff comes down. It would be nice if Santa was the beginning and end of it, but he's not. Disoriented birds fly down into the house and create Hitchcockian scenes of hysteria and mayhem. And every time it rains, expect a light spattering of diluted soot covering everything in the room. Your nice, pale room. Newly installed country dwellers always choose pale furnishings because they don't yet know about mud, soot, bugs and all the other troublesome mess just waiting to ruin their life. Or, at the very least, their carpet.

AGA IN DITCH

Reason 11: Agas

When I first saw my Aga, I did what the ancient and sacred rules of Aga ownership dictate, and instinctively parked my bottom against it. This was an infinitely pleasurable experience and, better still, delayed the moment when I would have to turn round, face the bugger and look on it not as a glorified radiator, but as a thing to cook on.

It was a terrifying prospect. I have been confronted by multiple slobbering Dobermanns and felt less fear. First, there was its size: Agas take up the sort of square metreage on which you could erect a decent-sized granny flat. And then there was its unassailable reputation. Saying nasty things – or even thinking less than complimentary thoughts – about an Aga is like implying the Pope is a filthy-mouthed, hard-drinking reprobate. Still, if what I'd heard from other, besotted Aga owners was correct – that I would fall in love with it on sight – then we were in for a long and happy relationship.

But – and maybe I have commitment issues here – I have never been in the habit of forming amorous attachments to kitchen appliances, and I struggled to see its allure. When, after four months, we had still failed to bond (does a counselling service exist for this sort of emotional blockage? I wondered), I turned to *Aga Magazine*, the popular fanzine for Aga owners.

Now, I suspect that if Agas were train sets and their owners men, subscribing to a publication such as this would attract accusations of anorakishness and nerdery of the very highest order. But because this is women and their cookers, they manage to get away with some of the most outrageous idolatry I have seen this side of the crowd barriers at a Barry Manilow concert.

I learned that, aside from splitting the atom and clearing up dog sick, there is virtually nothing an Aga can't do. It knew all about multi-tasking before the phrase had been invented. An Aga can simultaneously cook a roast dinner for 24 warm cold arses and revive semi-conscious hedgerow creatures. The magazine has a popular photo-gallery page that features peaky-looking pets (accompanied by 'amusing' captions) convalescing in the simmering oven. It has snapshots of women going though the early stages of labour butted up against the roasting-oven door. Maybe it's just me, but this strikes me as borderline sinister, like a kind of warped Readers' Wives scenario for the welly-wearing set.

Sixty-four pages of undiluted Aga-worship later, and still I felt unmoved by it on a deep, spiritual level. But what about on a superficial and entirely practical level? In other words, what was it like to cook on?

It was the only means of preparing hot food in the house, so after several weeks, during midwinter, on an enforced salad-heavy diet, I bit the bullet. In the beginning, when everything I attempted to cook turned out disastrously, I gave the Aga the benefit of the doubt. I blamed the cookery books, not the cooker. Jamie Oliver was an arse, Nigel Slater, plain vindictive, and Delia Smith a malicious-minded home-wrecker. While I struggled to get to grips with the Aga's inconsistent heat, erratic timing and rank spitefulness, I produced dried-out fish pies (Oliver), incinerated chocolate cakes (Slater), and toast that turned to cinders virtually on contact with the boiling plate (not strictly Delia's fault, but I'll go ahead and blame her anyway; I have a roll-call of Delia grievances going way back).

And then I discovered Mary Berry. Here was a woman who gazed out from the covers of her cookery books with the sort of authority and command that suggested she'd been through a lot of suffering in her quest to understand the mysterious ways of the Aga, and had emerged a scarred, but enlightened character. Anyway, I was desperate, and immediately warmed to her. It was that or put my head on the boiling plate and close the lid.

From the serene, unflappable look on Mary's face – part nun, part bereavement counsellor – it was clear that she had tamed her Aga in the same way a dog trainer placates a vicious terrier, and I needed her in my kitchen.

Through her books, she taught me patience and tolerance; she taught me that with an Aga, you have to get to know its foibles and idiosyncracies. You have to persist, in a non-threatening, non-violent manner, in your quest to understand its many quirks and individual personality traits to do with heat and timing.

But, all the same, forgive me if I decline to pledge undying love to it. I may now have a rudimentary grasp of how to cook something that is at least edible, but I still don't feel the need to seal this new relationship with the promise of lifelong commitment.

Or loyalty, for that matter. You see, I have a guilty secret. During a particularly low patch, when cakes would not rise, gratins would not brown and baked potatoes spontaneously combusted at the mere suggestion of being put into the roasting oven, I huffed off to Argos and bought a Baby Belling, a dinky cooker the size of a microwave oven, and a perennial favourite with space-poor pensioners and students. I then proceeded to create for myself what the Aga-faithful would see as a horribly shameful, two-ring bedsit scenario in the pantry. But what an oasis of culinary good sense this has turned out to be. What was originally intended as a short-term fix while I got to grips with the Aga, has triumphed in its role as indispensable fallback option. When I can't face the exhausting guesswork and uncertainty that comes with Aga ownership, I turn to my wonderfully consistent Baby Belling. It is dependable, unintimidating and reliable in a way an Aga will never be. I think I may even be a little bit in love.

Reason 12: Children

Not long after we had moved from London to Suffolk, I was driving one of my children's friends home and noticed that things had fallen very quiet in the back of the car. A quick glance in the rear view mirror showed my son and daughter gazing, rapt, out of their windows. A warm rush of relocation smuggery enveloped me. What had the newly ruralised little darlings noticed about their idyllic country surroundings? A frolicking lamb? A fascinating cloud formation? An intriguing example of roadside vegetation?

A couple of audible gasps and a 'Wow!' later, I asked them what they were looking at. This was surely something special. A sparrowhawk, perhaps, or, at the very least, a pair of boxing hares. By now, we had pulled into a cul-de-sac of anonymous new-builds a few miles from our house. Bikes were strewn across front gardens and kerbs, with children shouting and running all over the place. Caravans sat in driveways and, here and there, men were fiddling with motor bikes or cleaning their cars. 'This looks really good,' my children breathed, 'Why can't we live here?'

With a screech of tyres and a handbrake turn, I was out of there quicker than you could say Brookside Close. What the hell were the ungrateful wretches talking about? I had yet to hear them fawning quite so explicitly over our tree house, or the orchard and rolling lawn leading down to a river replete with ducks and sticklebacks. Hadn't we moved from our poky London terrace to a sprawling country pile expressly to give them fresh air and space to run around?

Hadn't we resolved to give them the outdoorsy and shoeless childhood experiences that would be denied them if we'd stayed in the city?

When we got home, I communicated my disappointment via a great deal of wordless door slamming and heavy sighing; whereas, later that evening, they were rather more articulate.

The lure of the cul-de-sac, it seemed, was that it looked as if it would be fun to live somewhere with other children close by, and a safe, largely traffic-free street to run around in. We, conversely, now lived in a huge, rather secluded and quiet detached house on the edge of the village, walled off from the road. The average age of our neighbours was 75. It was safe to assume that there would be no inter-garden ballgames any time soon; no whooping and yelling and running in and out of each others' houses trailing bikes and filth.

What about all the other things our house had going for it? I prompted the children, a little desperately. What about the original features, the period details, the rich history?

But who was I kidding? From a child's point of view, buying an old house when you can afford a new one just isn't logical. Why would any sane person want to do that? My daughter explained what it was that she liked about her new school-friend's modern house up the road in our village. It was bright, it was cosy and compact. No dark corners or mysteriously distant landings and corridors. Wherever you were in this girl's house, she said, you could hear what was going on in every other room; anathema to a peace-seeking adult, perhaps, but to a fearful child, endlessly reassuring. It was a good year after we moved in that my daughter finally stopped shadowing me everywhere I went, for fear of being left alone in what she regarded as a houseful of forebodingly cavernous and creepy rooms.

I wouldn't say the enormous garden was an instant hit, either. In London, the children were so used to being chaperoned everywhere they went, that the idea of running off to play on their own was a completely foreign, and daunting, idea. I recall that they warmed to the space and freedom at roughly the same time they started complaining about the glaring lack of tarmac surfaces on which to skateboard, ride bikes, and bounce balls.

Not for the first time, we were forced to confront the hypocrisy in having loudly trumpeted to anyone willing to listen that we were moving from London to the country for the sake of the children, while having completely neglected to canvas our children's opinions on any of the choices we had made.

But, at ages four and seven, weren't they too young to care, or even notice that we were moving away? Admittedly, we took the precaution of using stealth-relocation tactics, drip-feeding minimal information while telling ourselves they would effort-lessly adapt. We were wrong. They did notice, they did care, and for the first few months, they didn't embrace what we had moved to, but mourned what we had left behind.

The truth is that our vision of children roaming free and wholesome in their new rural world was hopelessly outdated. Prospective relocaters would do well to get their heads out of Enid Blyton and swot up instead on Melvyn Burgess's rather grittier and more realistic accounts of latter-day childhood, which include graphic exploration of sexual relationships and drug abuse for a modern teenage audience.

For a short while, your children may humour you by going

along with the vegetable patch thing, the egg-collecting lark, the running-barefoot-through-the-cornfield scenario that you wanted so badly for them. But very soon after they have rewarded you with what seemed like vindication of your relocation decision, they will completely reject it.

As they make local friends, it will become clear to them that rural children are not so very different from their urban counterparts in their likes and dislikes, and that you, with your airy-fairy ideas about country childhood, are making them look like freaks.

With this realisation, they will loudly announce that they're not remotely interested in rearing newborn chicks, making wormeries or growing their own pumpkins. Instead, they want to slump in front of the telly, play electronic games on the computer and loaf indolently around shopping precincts with their scrofulous friends.

You might think they've finally embraced life in the sticks when you see them spending long, lazy summer days swarming off along the lane in a happy, jostling herd with other local children – only to discover that they're sniffing glue down the playing fields while planning organised raids on the post office.

Crime and delinquency is very much alive in the countryside, usually fuelled by crushing boredom. Unless you are prepared to run a virtually round-the-clock, seven-day-a-week taxi service ferrying your children somewhere – anywhere – more interesting in the evenings and at weekends, expect problems when they're teenagers.

The fact is that children take a dim view of the quiet, restful lifestyle their parents covet. They only seem happy if opportunities for buying pizza and frapuccinos locally are many and plentiful. As they get older, they become increasingly scornful of rural events that pass for a social life in small communities. Barn dance, anyone? Folk singing, egg-rolling and a drive out to the next village for the shire-horse spectacular?

And they will be very vocal about their craving for amenities that aren't run by the WI and smell of mothballs and socks. Why can't they live in a noisy, bustling, built-up area with cinemas and shops, where life is more fun, there are other children to hang out with and their parents aren't so snobbish as to veto outdoor Christmas lights on the grounds that they're vulgar?

I think I can say with some assurance, then, that guilt about doing the right thing by your children doesn't evaporate with a new rural postcode and more space. It just takes on a new form. City parents worry about too much pollution, filth and crime; we now wring our hands about not enough cultural stimulation and too few opportunities for multi-racial interaction.

The ideal scenario that most relocating parents envisage

for themselves and their children is to maintain links with both city and countryside. Even if a lack of funds prohibits a dual existence, it's still the notion that persists at the back of their minds.

When it looks like too much plodding ruralism is having a deadening effect on their intellect, whisk the children off to town. When that noise and bustle looks like it's casting an indelible stain on their unblemished rural purity, rush them back to the country. A welly in one camp and a kick-ass brogue in the other.

Reason 13: The noise

Six years into our move to the country, I have found that leaving a city doesn't, after all, mean relocating to a place of complete silence and tranquility. It just means swapping one set of noises for another.

Most people think they know which ones they'd rather have. In an instant, they'd trade sirens, drunken late-night yelling, car horns and incessant traffic noise for babbling brooks, soothing bird-song and the gentle rustling of wind through the trees.

But those are just the country sounds that come to mind first – the kneejerk, greatest hits soundtrack to rural living. Check out the lesser known B-sides and hard-to-obtain rarities and you might find that not all country noises are especially attractive or tolerable.

Try pig farms, low-flying fighter jets from the local airfield, tiresome bird-scarers contrived to sound like gunshot, or the relentless chug of farm vehicles during harvest-time. Farmers are no respecters of traditional waking hours among sane and rational human beings (I'm guessing their reasoned thinking goes something like this: 'I'm up at 5am, knee-deep in sheep shit, so you lot can get up too, you idle buggers'), and their bloody-minded approach to timekeeping gets to you after a while.

Take the clock in our village square. When we first moved in, its hourly chime struck us as a quaint and cheering feature of village life. If this was as noisy as it got, what could we possibly find to complain about? For years, we had lived in close proximity to some of London's filthiest and most caco-phanous main roads.

If only the clock had had the good sense to belt up come nightfall, then it wouldn't have aroused any bad-tempered behaviour whatsoever. As it is, I have spent more nights than I care to number lying cursing in bed, listening to the pointless nocturnal chiming issuing from the square up the road.

The chief problem with some of the more insistent country sounds is that they only really crank into action just as you're trying to relax or get some sleep. It can be as silent as a graveyard all day, then almost the minute dusk falls, all hell lets loose. Randy ducks? Present and correct. Courting owls? We hear what you're saying. Local teenagers gathering under the street light to trade gutteral inanities? Receiving you loud and clear.

The row may then peter out as darkness comes, only to resume, with redoubled efforts, at sunrise. And while a heart-warmingly charming dawn chorus, beefed up by a distant cockerel, may be great once in a while, when it happens every day it can get a little wearing.

Spring is an especially challenging time for the noise-sensitive rural curmudgeon; in the country, animals are especially demonstrative at this sexually industrious time of year. More than a few times I have felt like leaning out of the window at an almost comically quack-filled 5am and yelling something along the lines of: 'I'm happy for you all, I really am, but could you just pipe down a bit? It's lovely that you're all getting along so famously, but some of us have jobs to go to. Now piss off.'

Ditto separation-anxiety-afflicted newborn lambs, demonstratively vocal cattle and, in general, loudly over-protective matriarchs of all species.

And don't assume that just because it's the countryside, there are no disaffected youths doing noisy things at night expressly to spread irritation and anger among the quiet-living. It's because they live in the country and are, therefore, doubly tanked up with boredom and frustration, that they feel the need to inflict especially irksome punishment on their neighbours. Empty country roads make great night-time race tracks. Remote, unsupervised community facilities are just asking to be loudly vandalised, and, come pub throw-out time, the effing and blinding of disgorged local teenagers carries beautifully down the deserted, echoey village streets.

But when it's quiet, it's very quiet. Which can create problems all of its own. You get accustomed to a certain level of silence – quiet, dead quiet and quieter still – that even the slightest noise can shatter. You know you've been in the country too long when the softest brush of willow branch against window pane assumes, to your newly sensitised ears, the decibel levels of a Red Arrows flypast. And a distant siren isn't just a distant siren, it's a sound that stops conversations, brings people out on to the street and fans the fire of the sort of outrageous rumour and speculation that sustains village gossip for weeks.

But there is one quintessentially rustic sound that is far and away more irritating, and ubiquitous, than all the others. Just as you are settling down in the garden to enjoy a rare lull in the virtually round-the-clock barrage of rural sound, it will be almost guaranteed that someone, somewhere, will be cranking a lawnmower or other piece of especially grating garden machinery into action.

Ironically, it's usually the people who are most protective of their peace and quiet – and quickest to complain about your dog/children/barbecues – who are the most obsessive about a tidy lawn and therefore generate the most noise. As they say in the city: go figure.

Reason 14: Country cottages

Before moving to the country, I had only very sketchy, romanticised ideas about what constituted the perfect country cottage. With no actual experience of rural life, these were ideas collected, over the years, from sources as diverse and unreliable as fuzzy pictures on the fronts of tea caddies, jigsaw box lids, Sunday evening television dramas set in West Country villages, and that scene in *Snow White* when a gang of industrious and ever so slightly irritating woodland creatures sets about spring-cleaning her house.

Later, these ideas were further embellished by visits to country house hotels. Through a mist of entrancement at the luxuriant drapery, the warming fires, the crumpets, the lavishly carpeted decadence and the fact that, at at least one of these places, there appeared to be a person employed solely to plump up cushions, we were sold on the idea.

Right from the start, out-of-town property agents seemed a lot more approachable than their sharkish counterparts in the city. And it wasn't just because of their benign casualwear and unintimidating way with a clipboard and blunt pencil. No, as we later realised, the warmly welcoming charm offensive was prompted, at least in part, by the fact that they like nothing more than a gullible townie couple in the first flush of relocation fever.

After lemmings and toddlers, such people are among some of the most naive, suggestible and wide-eyed creatures in christendom. Estate agents know this; they are well aware that, at some point en route from the city to a house viewing in the country, these couples' brains, and any accompanying capacity for sensible, rational thought, turn to mush, by way of pink marshmallow and fairy dust.

Their dreams – thatch dreams, half-timbered dreams, log fire and chintzy dreams – are built almost exclusively on seductive cosmetic detail and not the hard, often financially prohibitive realities that go with ownership of a house whose last brush with modernisation might easily have been around the time of mob caps and the Black Death.

Duly identified as just the latest in a long line of cash-rich, information-poor fantasists chasing the rural idyll, we embarked on our search. We were shepherded around a number of country properties and cooed and swooned appreciatively. Blind to any failings, we noted only the good points.

We saw wonderful leaded windows, not crumbling sills. We noticed the lovely thatch, not the rotting gables. Where there was worm-riddled infrastructure, we saw only appealing beamwork. And even if the occasional flaw did catch our attention, we were endlessly forgiving. Wasn't there romance and charm in rural decrepitude? Wasn't there something socially and historically rich about rustic degeneration? Surely these imperfections spoke of the intricacies of centuries-old social fabric and interesting lives led, in a way that leaky plumbing and bad tilework in characterless new-builds categorically didn't?

And how fabulous, we told ourselves, to get away from the grinding predictability of London terraces. How refreshing to approach a front door and know nothing of the architectural riches that lay inside. Unlike a Victorian townhouse, where the layout varies minutely and, give or take a modernising knock-through here and there, a loft conversion or some claim-back-a-bit-of-much-needed-daylight jiggery-pokery with that useless bit of passageway down the side, all are more or less the same.

It was after our twentieth or so viewing that, like cracked tiles off a knackered roof, the scales fell from our eyes, and we called in Brian the relocation agent to do the looking for us. We finally arrived at the conclusion that stooping down to pass through yet another miniature, Alice in Wonderland-style front door wasn't charming or quaint, it was irritating, depressing and, frankly, unnatural.

I mean, who exactly were these houses built for? If, based on their proportions, you were to piece together a demographic profile, then you would have to surmise that the average cottage dweller was a three-foot midget with a mole's appreciation of dark tunnelly places, a total disregard for any sort of personal hygiene, and a constitution that could withstand damp, sub-zero temperatures and still have enthusiasm left for risking their life daily on staircases conceived with especially deft-hooved mountain goats in mind.

In fact, many of these cottages were inhabited by farmworkers who spent much of their time outdoors. They were built with only very basic functionality in mind, and adequate natural light was not a priority (by all accounts, glass was prohibitively expensive, so windows were kept small).

The notion of comfort was given barely a thought; it's probably fair to say that the sheep-shearers and sugar beet harvesters of East Anglia weren't overly preoccupied with this season's chintzy rose-print upholstery or trends in lightshade trimmings. The stone-floored, freezing cold, dank inhospitability was perhaps why they very sensibly moved out of these squalid dumps just as soon as they got the chance, and why they would surely laugh like drains at the prices these places now command, and the covetability they enjoy.

But adapting them to modern needs is far from straightforward. Leaving aside height and sanitary issues, just to attain a decent-sized room is often difficult. Beams, central chimneys and thick interior walls don't readily lend themselves to the middle-class, open-plan ideal. Although it doesn't stop people trying – during our search, we witnessed a great many desperate, often hopelessly botched attempts at carving viable living space out of dark, warren-like interiors.

Our original wish-list, then, which included, in order of priority, exposed beams, leaded windows and cosy inglenooks was amended to read absolutely no beams, lose the hideously small windows and forget cosiness. Cosy had become a byword for poky and we wanted none of it.

In the end, we ignored all the lessons we'd learned about perilous antiquity and the high-risk strategy of investing in a house built in the 1400s, and bought a huge, sprawling money-pit that is way too big and draughty, has any number of leaks, creaks and rotting timberwork, and floors so uneven that to walk the length of the upstairs landing is like being on the upper deck of a permanently listing cross-Channel ferry.

The house did at least excel in performing its primary purpose: that of persuading me, by virtue of its heartbreaking gorgeousness, that leaving London was a good idea, and not, in fact, an act of extreme folly by a dyed-in-the-wool townie with absolutely no affinity for rural life. However, even when you find the house of your dreams, there is no guarantee that you will be content in it for long. In London, one house was much like another, but in the country, the variety is enormous. There are so many achingly pretty cottages around, owned by house-proud show-offs keen to flaunt their spruced and trimmed gardens, thatches and delightful half-timbering, that you can't help but have your head turned.

The symptoms of cottage-envy can creep up almost imperceptibly. First you might vaguely note that someone else's wisteria is, this year, flourishing a whole lot better than yours. Then you could start to nurse a twinge of envy that another neighbour's mullion windows are altogether more attractive and authentic-looking than those in your house. Before you know it, you are starting to do borderline irrational things such as drive around the lanes in the hours of darkness, staking out other people's cottages and noting, with barely concealed outrage and jealousy, that this lot here have their own moat! Or a pond with divine lilies and ducklings! Or, for pity's sake, a paddock out the back with grazing horses!

You might then thunder home in a fury of covetousness at the knowledge that your house, the house you took to be the most picture-perfect in Suffolk, is, in fact, more than a few fondant creams short of the full chocolate box.

Competitive cottagery is not an admirable quality in the rural dweller. It is grubby, destructive and a little shameful. It's nice to be proud of your little bit of history and all, but get a grip: keep it in proportion.

I hope I'm never driven to obsessively hanker after a neighbour's bressamer beam or fabulously ornate chimney stack, although I have recently heard it through the grapevine that a place in the next village is flaunting a particularly fine new paint-job on its ornate Tudor porch.

I am itching to go and have a look, but I shall resist making a special journey, because I'd like to think I have my house-stalking habit under control. Kerb crawling past adorable cottage gardens, staring slack-jawed at immaculate picket fences, or sitting in a car outside someone else's house for long stretches for the purpose of longingly sizing up their exemplary brickwork may be perfectly innocent in intention, but I doubt it would hold water in court.

Reason 15: Moaning

I used to think I was pretty good at moaning – I once reduced a BT operator to tears, and received £25 in supermarket vouchers after a sustained campaign against over-long check-out queues. But then I moved to the country and realised that, out here, the business of complaining is cranked up to a whole new level. City dwellers may excel at quickfire, rapid-response rage, but here, they specialise in the sort of slow-burning, festering whingeing that requires dedication, stamina and real creative talent to pull off.

East Anglia provides fertile ground for the career moaner: for a start, there's the long-running row about the extra runway at Stansted – always good for a couple of evenings a week's organised grouching, and a protest march or two. Then there's the proposed building of a swathe of wind farms across the area, a subject that is never more than a turbine's width away from a lengthy feature slot on *Anglia News*. A few years ago, Maggi Hambling's enormous scallop sculpture on Aldeburgh beach enraged neophobic locals. With these and other rumblings of disquiet ticking over on a pretty much continual basis, there's more than enough material to keep the region's parish council meetings humming for months to come.

Anyone who doubts these impressive feats of sustained disgruntlement need only turn to the letters page of the *East Anglian Daily Times* – the first refuge of the apoplectic, the angry and the merely pissed off. To read these daily outpourings of bile and fury, you would have to surmise that East Anglians live in a perpetual state of boiling rage at the antics of those jumped up sods from the city – led by a 'hopelessly metrocentric' government – and their 'relentless crusade' to, basically, 'shut the countryside down'.

That's right: pull down the blinds and turn out the lights. To start with, 'they' will shut its post offices, its schools and bring an already 'pitifully inadequate' public transport to its knees. And if they don't succeed in 'closing the place down completely' – the countryside takes up too much space, makes a woeful contribution to the GDP, and is riddled with resource-leaching old people – they can, at the very least, sanction its ruination with the erection of any number of 'breathtakingly ugly monuments to modernism and progress'.

Given this roll-call of grievances, is it any surprise that the gentle rural citizen is tearing its collective hair out?

You'd think all this moaning would make for an insufferable climate of misery and curmudgeonliness but, on the contrary, people are buoyant, motivated and, it seems, more than sustained by the need to complain on a pretty much continual basis about anything and everything.

Perhaps in a more urban climate, this sort of dogged negativity would earn you a reputation as an insufferable bore but, out here, moaning doesn't make you unpopular – it earns you respect as a dedicated front-line soldier in the ongoing battle against the march of progress and anything loud or unattractively modern that might theoretically threaten the future of your thatch, your mullion windows, your tranquility or your unbroken view across picturesque farmland.

And, as I soon discovered when I moved here, incomers would be well advised to observe the unspoken rules of rural grumbling. For a start, you must be open and generous with your whingeing: communal griping is the glue that binds villages together, and the first step to successful integration is to establish, in full view of other villagers, your credentials as a world-class complainer. The person who moans alone stays alone, and that just isn't healthy.

This means being prepared to discuss openly, in the doctor's waiting room, the full and unexpurgated details of whatever ailment has brought you there. Being coy will earn you accusations of stand-offishness and snobbery, and that's not what you want when you're trying to integrate.

It goes without saying that, even before you have left the surgery, the nuts and bolts of your compromised physical health will have gone up and down the village high street like an STD round a brothel.

But this is a good thing. Keeping secrets won't make you any friends in a village. To be open, blabbery, blurty and, above all, fabulously indiscreet, is to be the most sought after gossip-buddy anyone could hope for.

And when a villager greets you and asks you how you are (even though they clearly couldn't give a toss; they're just being nosy), they don't want to hear 'fine' or 'very well, thank you'. Forget the clipped, cursory exchanges that passed for mutually empathetic discourse back in London: these people want to hear bad things, long-winded tragic things, great rambling tirades about how miserable you are and how difficult you're finding it to settle in and make friends. This sort of one-on-one heartfelt outpouring counts as very high-calibre moaning indeed, and will earn you a great many brownie points along the road to acceptance into the community.

It's worth remembering that there is no gripe too petty or

piffling for a public airing; also, as well as dishing out the complaints, when you move into a village you must be prepared to be on the receiving end of opprobrium.

My first brush with local disapproval came a few months after we'd moved in. We were prominently named and shamed in the village magazine which, despite its unassuming A5 size, interminable detailing of parish council minutes and strange adverts for catteries and mobile hairdressers, may as well be the *New York Times* for the clout it carries locally. And while I realise being exposed by a monthly periodical stapled together by members of the WI doesn't necessarily measure up to being outed in a broadsheet-style investigative scoop, it was crushing nevertheless.

Our crime? A Virginia creeper had, apparently, worked its way over the garden wall and was now 'compromising the safe passage of dog-walkers up the road adjacent to the church'. That it would only compromise your passage if you were twelve foot wide and built like a Martello tower was beside the point. The situation had been reported to the parish council and treated, it seemed, with the same grave disapproval that greets unprovoked assaults on pensioners, hit-and-run incidents, and arson.

Then there was the case of the Japanese knotweed that garnered a chilling anonymous leaflet detailing its shortcomings as a deadly garden parasite. That was followed swiftly by a letter from the local council's environmental health officer pointing out the dangers of allowing such a wayward and virulent horticultural hazard to ramble unchecked through my garden.

On the grand scale of disasters, not very disastrous, but to some old codger with too much time on his hands, I had planted a seed of disgruntlement and that seed had grown into a gripe; the gripe had mushroomed into a grievance which had then found its way on to paper and into the in-tray of a council official. Now, I would have been perfectly happy to discuss the whole creeping-overhangy thing with the aggrieved party face to face, but face to face isn't the way things happen in villages. In villages, people like to follow The Right Channels. Not least because kick-starting a lot of bureaucracy and paperwork ensures that the grievance is prolonged, extended and, with any luck, is likely to involve a frenetic volley of official letters.

After six years here, I have learned that moaning is contagious, like nits and Anthrax. Bitching begets bitching, gossip fuels more gossip and before you know where you are, you are infected along with everyone else.

Recently I found myself standing in the village shop, face like a slapped arse, arms folded across my chest, ranting furiously about the scandal of the village square's decommissioned phone box, last December's overly vulgar Christmas decorations and the barely tolerable noise (some loud amens, a cheerio and a few ear-piercing God bless you's) made by departing worshippers from the church next door.

And to think that, when I lived in London, I was in an area where people would routinely deal drugs on our doorstep, chase each other down the road with machetes, dump dead goat carcasses in our garden, and set fire to our dustbins. I seem to remember that these nightly disturbances and gross acts of anti-socialness barely even registered with us, much less provoked complaint.

So why have I become so intolerant? I used to like vulgar Christmas lights. What do I care if there's a phone box or not?

I'd like to think that my recently acquired talent for carping is symptomatic of the sense of protectiveness and pro-prietorial civic pride that goes hand in hand with living in beautiful surroundings. Essentially, we rural villagers feel lucky, blessed and fortunate and are simply defending our little patch of paradise.

Either that or we're all insufferable, small-minded grouches with too much time on our hands.

Reason 16: The smell

If you have ever been downwind of an Estee Lauder counter, spent any time at all browsing the rails at Sue Ryder, have a working knowledge of nappy-changing procedures or are in regular contact with tinned petfood, then you will know what it is to wince with violent olfactory distaste. But you haven't truly winced until you have spent a long hot summer in the countryside.

There seems to be a prevailing belief that country smells are somehow more benign and acceptable than smells that issue from man-made urban sources. But, like the sinister-looking sludge that oozes and bubbles in the puddles and troughs of the region's pigsties, this belief is, largely, rot and codswallop.

The traditional picture of the contented country dweller

is not of someone going around holding their nose and grimacing horribly, perhaps covering their face with a scarf while attempting to contain the urge to retch, but, nevertheless, in the height of the stinky season – or summer, as it's sometimes known – it's the only way to get by.

And by stinky I'm not referring to straight manure. Compared to the stuff that passes as fertiliser these days, manure is as fragrant as Mary Archer's knicker drawer. As for cowpats, I now file them in the same nostalgia memory bank (subheading: pleasantly evocative smells) as buttered crumpets and old ladies' lavender bags.

I don't, and probably wouldn't want to know, the exact components of the rotted-down animal matter they put on the fields round here, but from the whiffs that penetrate my makeshift facial mask, it's a fair guess that: 1) it hails from the sea, possibly by way of Helm's Deep and the Seventh Circle of Hell, and 2) that it has not taken a living breath for an exceptionally long time.

You don't want to think too hard about the wisdom/ethics/health implications of having this horrendous, otherworldly slurry heaped on to fields full of crops destined for your local shops, your fridge and, ultimately, your stomach, but you can't help wondering.

Chemical sprays and pesticides are another olfactory blight on rural summers. For the time being, in our house anyway, the physical side effects are restricted to violent hay fever and sundry other respiratory problems much worse than anything we experienced when exposed to London pollution.

But I wouldn't be the first person to admit to a suspicion that the true implications of these substances will only be known 30 years down the line, when we start growing extra heads, develop huge suppurating sores over 80 per cent of our bodies, and notice an unnatural growth of excess body hair (notwithstanding the high proportion of rural folk who already look like this and who don't have modern farming methods to blame).

You leave the city to escape adverse reactions to noxious air-bound matter, and you walk straight into the rural blight that is rapeseed. It's a sneaky one, this. It wears its pungent nastiness beneath a gorgeously flamboyant outer layer of dramatic yellow. It is, literally, breathtaking, inspiring both awe and chronic wheezing in equal measure.

For people pre-disposed to hating farmers, it's yet more grist to the resentment mill. On top of all the other irritations – slow-moving farm vehicles all over the roads during summer, needlessly loud bird-scarers at anti-social times of day, grain lorries hurtling down our narrow village street at 6am, hostility towards ramblers, general surliness in the face of non-farming country folk trying to enjoy country life even though they don't pay their dues by standing knee-deep in pig shit all day – they inflict smells on us at the very time of year we want to fling open the windows and be outside.

Farmers have made it their business to ensure that these nasty smells are so very nasty that the memory of them stays fresh in the nostrils long after the air has cleared and made way for something more tolerable. That's how mean-minded they are.

Reason 17: Schools

When I lived in London, it was as much a staple dinner-party feature as votive candles, Nigella puddings and earnest agonising about allergies and food intolerances. It was a topic that would invariably come up long before the coffee hit the table, and sometimes even pre-starter. It would exercise guests long into the night, even more than the Chardonnay versus Sauvignon Blanc debate, the efficacy of the cabbage soup diet, and the wisdom of investing in a second home in Bulgaria.

It was the troubling Schools question, and it got people into a right lather. The general agreement was that the local primary schools were just about alright, but after that, you were up shit-creek. There were three stark choices. Abandon your principles and go private, put your faith in a failing inner-city secondary, or subject your child to a three-hour daily round-trip to a far-flung, edge of London comprehensive (assuming you could negotiate catchment area issues).

Alternatively, you could move out. While your children were still small and relatively untainted by the vagaries of the London education system and before it became routine for schools to employ armed doormen to search pupils for drugs and firearms.

Doesn't every disillusioned townie parent have a picture in their heads of the idyllic rural primary school set-up? Think about it: the interminable school-run would no longer be a run, but a leisurely, calm, five-minute stroll – down a farm track bordering cornfields. It would involve absolutely no belching SUVs, traffic jams, parking tickets or road rage altercations involving foul-mouthed bike messengers and bendy buses.

Class sizes would be small, and the school cosy and intimate, with pastoral care right at the top of its priorities. All things considered, wouldn't it be a bit like having an exclusive, free, private school directly on your doorstep?

In our wistful imaginings, the typical village school was an adorable, old-fashioned Victorian establishment in the heart of the village, with a safe playground featuring, perhaps, painted hopscotch squares and a handful of fabulously carefree-looking local children dressed in pinafores, chasing hoops around (alright, perhaps that's a fantasy too far) and with no working knowledge of some of the more X-rated latter-day profanities or brain-rottingly gormless texting techniques.

Other rumblings of discontent sprang from the fact that while our children's London school was great at teaching them how to splash paint around and do previously unimagined things with pulses and polystyrene packing materials, its grasp of basic teaching was lamentable. And while school-gate culture was great for us – a colourful and eclectic set of creative parents from the worlds of media and the arts meant that drop-off and pick-up times were never dull – perhaps it was about time we started to think about whether our children were going to leave school with anything more useful than a working knowledge of kite-making and yurt-construction. Needlessly meddlesome PC initiatives began to irritate. Scrapping sports day and turning it into the less divisive 'infant challenge day' grated badly. A liberal approach that frowned on uniform, formal titles for teachers, and, it seemed, any structured work whatsoever, wasn't looking delightfully relaxed anymore – just flaky.

With all this in mind, and after months spent agonising over a copy of the *Telegraph Good Schools Guide*, we duly enrolled our children at the village school. It was, we felt sure, the right decision; they would quickly make local friends and feel safer and more secure than they had done in their vast London primary.

The first surprise was that the school did not inspire the loyalty of every parent in the village. Children catching buses to at least ten different private schools in the region were very much in evidence in the square each morning (though our research showed that the high school in the next town that our children would attend at secondary level was highly regarded).

It was beginning to dawn on us that the rural system did not have all the answers. For a start, the compact intimacy and low head count that first entrances the city exile has the disadvantage of garnering fewer government resources. And if your child doesn't get along with the handful of children in his or her often mixed-age year, there is less choice of alternative playmates than there would be in a bigger school. Another eye opener was that not every country child is a rosy-cheeked angel raised on home-baking and fresh air. No. There are horrid, badly behaved children in the country just as there are in the city, only here, in a small community, they're harder to avoid.

One of my son's first regretful looks back to his old school was for his diverse mix of friends from countries such as Iran and the Gambia. Where were their equivalents here? I could see him wondering, as he looked, bemused, at a wholly alien concentration of exclusively white faces. And where was the breakneck round of after-school activities they were used to in London? I had to admit, I missed it myself. City parents moan about the never-ending circuit of tap and ballet, tennis and music lessons, but when they are submerged deep in the often lonely netherworld of childcare, meeting other parents on the treadmill of extra-curricular school activities can fill the gaps in a pitifully diminished adult social life.

I tried to see the less demanding pace as a good thing. This was a far gentler, more old-fashioned and less pushy approach to schooling. Without the infectious, high-octane neurosis and chivvying that went with urban parenting, there would be more time for our children to play with friends and generally hang out at home. It would be good for them.

In return, they would receive that precious reward I had heard other misty-eyed ex-urbanite parents talk about: the gift of prolonged childhood. Thanks to the countryside and its more wholesome, slower outlook, they would stay younger for longer, and that could only be good.

Until, of course, we started hearing from London friends about their children's latest feats of precociousness. The nine-year-old who was blithely travelling across town alone by underground each day to attend her acclaimed city prep-school. Or the twelve-year-old who had just formed his own band playing Nirvana covers, and had a series of London-wide gigs lined up. Or the kid who had the wherewithal to put himself up for a competition that would see him flying unaccompanied to Barcelona to visit a top-flight design consultancy.

Meeting up with an old friend and his family in London recently, the venue he'd picked for lunch was a Japanese restaurant. While our children made not very subtle faux-puking faces and enquired loudly after the availability of pasta, his daughters (younger than ours) calmly ordered smoked yakatori eel and embarked on a lengthy, informed cross-table discussion about the indigenous bird-life of Costa Rica.

I'm not saying only urban kids can achieve these things, or that city living and outrageous self-confidence necessarily go hand in hand, or that it's not just all our fault for having been crap parents and fail to instill in our children, wherever we live, similar qualities of self-assuredness and worldy nous.

But these instances of what we understood to be exclusively urban poise and maturity on the part of these London-raised children seemed always to come during a trough of rural disillusionment, and highlighted just how immature and un-thrusting our own children appeared by comparison.

They weren't playing thrash metal and piercing their noses; they were watching *Blue Peter* and singing in the school choir. They weren't doing battle on public transport during rush hour in a busy city, they were barely street-wise enough to walk to the village shop alone. They wouldn't, and in all likelihood never will, consider eel a viable menu option.

Was this all because we had wrenched them away from a city that promised a rich, rounded and adventurous upbringing, to make them live in the countryside and face a future as bumbling know-nothings with zero ambition?

It's at sweaty, panicky times like these that I come over all Hallmark and seek solace in the thought that childhood is a fleeting and precious thing and should be joyous, carefree and unpressurised. There is, surely, all the time in the world for rock-band-forming, cross-city-trekking and eel-experimentation.

Until then, they have my blessing to fool around, laugh and play like the backward (or delightfully innocent and well-adjusted) rurally-raised children they are, and enjoy it while it lasts.

Reason 18: People-watching

I wonder if that prison warder from *Bad Girls* noticed me staring at her while she was looking at bras in the Ipswich branch of M&S? Did she sense she was being trailed around the thermal section, or stalked in nightwear? In the event, no security guards were called and the incident passed without serious consequence, but I shocked even myself. The sheer length of time I spent on surveillance, feigning interest in support hose and control pants, signalled to me that I've been too long out of the game and am missing the rush.

The game I refer to is the intoxicating sport of celebrity-spotting; the accompanying blood-surge is the thrill that comes with getting a snatched glimpse of someone off the telly doing something fabulously mundane such as catching a bus, waiting in a supermarket queue or ordering a skinny latte from Caffè Nero.

When I lived in London, the streets were heaving with marginally well-known, averagely celebrated, and sometimes madly famous, faces going about their business for the delectation of inveterate gawpers like me. It was bliss. You could be stepping out on what promised to be just another humdrum weekday morning, and there, at the tube station, would be some bit-part auxiliary nurse from *Holby City*, or a fairly inconsequential desk-jobsworth from *Prime Suspect*. It could turn a mediocre day into a special one, it could put a spring in your step and a smile on your face.

Here in the country, there is no such fertile stomping ground for the dedicated star-spotter. In the six years I have been in Suffolk, my league table remains unrevised (Charlotte Rampling, Harvey Nichols, 1989, still at the top; Michael Ignatieff, buying liver sausage in Tesco, 1998, languishing at the bottom) and my personal library of sightings has grown by just one.

To give you an idea of just how desperate the situation is, the local paper recently conducted a poll to name the top ten most famous East Anglians. Studying the results, I think we can safely assume I won't be spotting John Constable or Benjamin Britten across the tinned fish aisle at Tesco any time soon.

When John Peel died, I was more cross than upset. He lived just up the road and, in local terms, was virtually papal in the devotion and adoration and crowd-worship he commanded. His death has rendered an already pathetic star-count even more diminished.

All right, if I were really gagging for a fix, I could seek out Delia Smith. But eyeballing Delia would involve a good hour's drive and a lot of hanging around Norwich City football ground. This would not fit into the category of chance encounter. This would constitute the sick, premeditated behaviour of an unstable person with no life. Besides, while up that way, I might accidentally bump into Bernard Matthews, and that wouldn't be at all nice.

So I have had to look elsewhere for my thrills. Some months back, when I was sulkily pondering why none of the cast of *Casualty* lives anywhere near the A12, I saw a weasel skittering along the bank of the river that runs through our garden. I would like to be able to say that the adrenaline surge it triggered was not unadjacent to the kind of buzz I'd experience if I were butted up against Jude Law in the queue at the post office, and that the last time I felt my pulse quicken this significantly was when I saw two detectives from *Silent Witness* at King's Cross station back in 1990.

Since the weasel, things have mushroomed, sightings-wise. I have notched up several grass snakes, a litter of leverets and a fallow buck. A kingfisher regularly swoops down the river diving for sticklebacks, and a great spotted woodpecker and a sparrowhawk are frequent visitors to the garden.

In celebrity terms, this abundance of A-list wildlife is like all Max Clifford's Christmases come at once. It's Richard Desmond's fantasy edition of *OK!* There's enough star material here to keep the 3am girls employed for the rest of their lives, and yet I remain unmoved by this veritable galaxy of winged and four-legged stars.

All very heartwarming seeing a moorhen and her chicks, but it seems no real substitute for spotting Bill Nighy leaving Sketchley with his dry-cleaning. And I can't help still feeling that I'd rather be hanging around outside Nobu on the off-chance of catching a glancing back view of a premiership footballer than watching an unsuspecting badger blundering out of the hedgerow. Let it go, I tell myself. I am not in London anymore. I must put behind me the puerile, shallow and frankly idiotic hankerings that city living fostered in me.

But I am rubbish at country life. It's too slow, it's too quiet, and since Lovejoy finished filming in a market town not far near here over a decade ago, there has been precious little action on the thespian front.

I was not cut out to be a connoisseur of animal droppings. I am very unlikely to turn into a fanatical twitcher complete with binoculars and a folded-up Ordnance Survey map in a waterproof plastic pouch.

Besides, there is little kudos in notching up, say, your fifth fox cub in a week. No one who isn't called Bill Oddie wants to hear about it; whereas, if you say you've just seen the tall one from *Friends* in a Covent Garden hotel lobby, everyone is transfixed.

On the other hand, life would be a lot easier – I would experience a lot less inner conflict and turmoil – if I could just surrender to the pull of nature, buy myself a many-pocketed khaki explorer's jacket and start to regard animals with new enthusiasm. Look at the advantages of being in the country, away from celebrity temptation and all the attendant tat. Animals do not have expensive gossip magazines devoted to them, and are a lot less risky in terms of stalking litigation.

The beauty of wildlife-watching seems to be that you can do all this prowling around without risk of a restraining order or being put on a stoat-botherers' register. Police will not come round and confiscate your vast library of literature and videos, or brand you sick in the head for having walls plastered with revealing, furry close-ups downloaded from the internet.

Instead of blatant nosy-parkering, prying rural-style is called curiosity and healthy interest. Or so they say. Having read some of the literature, with accompanying author photographs, in a recent copy of *Wildlife Watch* magazine, I'm not entirely convinced that the men out here with their beady eyes and utility slacks are fundamentally any less creepy than their London-based paparazzi counterparts.

Reason 19: Craft shops

When I heard there was a thriving, popular craft shop and tea-room in the next village, I was out of the house quicker than you could say basketweave desk-tidy. I wasn't so naive as to imagine it would be Harvey Nichols reworked for a pinny and pot-holder clientele, but I was excited nevertheless. This was how shop-starved I had become after three years in the retail desert. Unless you like agricultural machinery or pig feed, there is little else to buy within a half-hour radius of our house, and I was keen to reacquaint myself with the heady rush that comes from a hard cash transaction, the muscular whirr of the till, the crackle of tissue paper and even the grunt of a monosyllabic interaction with a surly teenage sales assistant. I missed it all, and I needed a fix, even if that fix was knitted, or woven, or crafted from wool harvested from the downy underbellies of locally reared lambs. And then dyed rust.

Barely five minutes in, and I was afflicted with what regular visitors to such places would immediately recognise as Craft Shop Stoop, a temporary but painful alteration in posture brought on by having to bend virtually double to avoid the many dangling, hairy, crocheted obstacles that hinder smooth passage through the cramped aisles.

The other people in the shop – coachloads of them, if the heaving car park was anything to go by – seemed wholly un-deterred by such hindrances. They were in no hurry. I have seen lamp-posts travel faster. They were happy to shuffle and loiter and, in some cases, submit to the trance-like state brought on by prolonged exposure to mind-altering scented candle emissions, pan-pipe music, and the all-pervading whiff of semi-hardened craft glue.

Is it desirable, or even legal, to do that sort of thing with driftwood, fuse wire and dried peas? I wondered, as I picked a route through the perilously cluttered shelves. What kind of person would think of marrying abstract chicken-wire sculpture with striped pipecleaners? Britain's chief rural export may be potatoes, but based on the clamour for the tills I witnessed that day, those spuds have close rivals in amusingly shaped draught-excluders, miniature seascapes painted on pebbles, and cushions embroidered with droll aperçus about the behaviour of cats.

The appetite for this stuff, it seems, is insatiable. Craft shops are to rural towns and villages what Costa Coffee is to airport concourses. They are everywhere, working the idyllic cottage theme – ostentatiously groomed thatch, adorably dimpled bow windows and overfilled hanging baskets – and with whimsical names that speak of infantile literary references (Mrs Tiggywinkle's tea-room) or a desperate need to evoke Lilliputian imagery (Thimbles), for fear that tourists will be frightened off by anything big and grown up and which looks like it might – whisper it – serve some functional purpose.

Small, fiddly, miniature stuff is craft shop gold. Microscopic pottery cottages, tiny village scenes embroidered on to bookmarks, miniscule matchstick-art barely visible to the human eye, is to the average craft shop what massproduced, drip-dry copies of the Turin shroud are to pilgrims of Bethlehem.

Visitors are endlessly forgiving of the outrageous tat that masquerades as saleable giftware. It's the same sort of retail delusion that sees British travellers to Greece bringing back Retsina. On holiday, in the sun, it was God's own nectar. Once home, under a relentlessly gloomy sky, it tastes remarkably like month-old dog urine. The same with craft-shop tourists. At home in town, they wouldn't dream of buying a set of coasters made from rough-hewn cross-sections of tree bark, decorated with shells, then varnished; but here under the persuasive spell of rural craft-shop magic, they seem so right.

After small things, homemade fudge and personalised trinketry (never let it be said that the desire to have your name on your pen, keyring, notebook begins and ends at primary school) animal themes form the mainstay of craft shop custom. Wind-chimes wrought to resemble a cat and its five dangling kittens beckon in visitors as surely as if it were a call to prayer. The craft-shop faithful stay in there for hours at a time, and it's a mystery as to why.

Perhaps, to these urban out-of-towners, craft shops represent a soft, down-filled world of hedgehoggy innocence behind which lies a wholly unchallenging marketing initiative. No one is hurrying you along. There is no pressure to buy. Craft shops lack the hard-bitten venality of urban retailers, where profit and cash flow mean everything. Visitors from town clearly like the soporific, coma-inducing state brought on by questionable pot-pourri mixes and things stuffed with lavender.

Perhaps, for us locals, the most irritating thing about craft shops is that, in already choice-impoverished rural areas, they occupy retail space that could surely be better used – Tesco Metro anyone?

When push comes to shove, an amusing wall plaque

detailing the hilarious peccadilloes of your pet collie will not sustain you in the way a loaf of bread and a decent bottle of red would.

Reason 20: Lawns

Things we didn't take into consideration before we moved to the country, number 3,452: during the spring and summer, when gardens grow, they require an enormous amount of upkeep and labour; the sort of upkeep and labour that we didn't have the competence, motivation, or time to take on. Contrary to some very skewed strands of thought that must have propelled us towards the purchase of a sprawling two acres, weeds don't pull themselves up, dead leaves don't assemble themselves into orderly piles when autumn ends, and lawns have not yet learned to mow themselves. There is no pruning elf who magically appears ready to dead head the roses when it's all over for another year.

But what did we know? This was the first proper garden

we'd ever had. Up until now, it had been small concrete back-yards all the way, backyards that always responded in an unswervingly positive manner to all the neglect we could throw at them.

Now things were different. Now, neglect wasn't an option. The garden we had inherited was huge and immaculate; amid the rolling lawns and well-stocked beds, it had a dovecote, a gazebo, numerous rose-bowers and a summer house, all bisected with a prettily gurgling river and a weeping willow supporting a wooden swing that wouldn't disgrace a Fragonard masterpiece.

There were large numbers of specimen trees, a croquet lawn, a lovely orchard, a great many rare plants and a neat kitchen garden, all planned and maintained to a high standard with an enormous amount of hard work, skill and devotion. Unsurprisingly, the garden featured prominently on the must-see list of the National Open Gardens scheme, and the pressure to keep it ship-shape felt very great indeed.

There was a two-month gap between having our offer accepted and exchanging contracts and, as we discovered to our horror, two months is an exceptionally long time in gardening. Two months is the difference between nicely trimmed grass and a wayward, frondy jungle. It's the difference between pristine, weeded beds and unholy horticultural mayhem.

By the time we moved in, things had slipped badly – the weeds were out of control, the grass knee-high, the compost heap was bulging and there were fallen leaves everywhere. Mild panic took hold. Perhaps we should also have been disappointed that the black swans, the peacocks, the gypsy caravan and all the Eduardo Paolozzi statuary had departed with the previous owners, but in fact we were relieved: it meant less stuff to worry about.

It came as a sobering realisation, but we were completely unaccustomed to any sort of free-form natural vegetation. Parched office plants and dusty corporate window boxes, yes. Municipal hanging-basketry and neat, central-reservation box-hedging certainly. But nothing more rampant than that. We had seen pitifully little of nature in the raw, unless you count the odd example of fridge-mould and the primal mating rituals of Northern Line passengers travelling on the last tube home.

In the city, nature doesn't need controlling; it is stopped in its tracks long before it becomes a problem. Here in the countryside, we encountered no such helpful curtailment; in our garden alone, evidence of nature's rampant, unfettered wilfulness was everywhere.

To preserve our sanity, our mental health and, to an extent, our relationship, something – anything – needed wrestling into submission.

And that something turned out to be the lawn.

As seems to be the ancient and unarguable law of lawn-maintenance, my husband took control. Along with bonfires and woodpiles, lawns are an aspect of nature that men feel comfortable squaring up to. Mother Nature is, after all, female, and women gaining the upper hand where fire, wood and grass growth are concerned has a deeply emasculating effect on modern men.

Besides which, slashing and burning are tried and tested domestic methods of domination and triumph. Men steer clear of taking on the wilder, less tangible aspects of nature such as weather and death, because they know they've got absolutely no chance of winning. Give them stuff to torch or cut down, on the other hand, and they are assured a victorious outcome.

And so, a year into our move, the lawn looked velvety soft and as neat as a squaddie's crew-cut. With the grass brought under control, everything else took on a less unruly aspect. Looking at the lawn, you could almost imagine that this garden was the work of people with half an idea about what they were doing. You'd think this horticultural breakthrough with the lawn would, henceforth, bring us nothing but pure pleasure.

But this has turned out to be far from true. Instead of sitting out on it and appreciating its deliciously vibrant colour, its springiness, its smell, and its gently undulating slope down to a prettily gurgling river, we seem to spend an awful lot of time perched uncomfortably on its gravel periphery, unwilling to besmirch its immaculate expanse with anything so ruinously vulgar as footsteps, and pondering the vexing issue of stripes.

Not since my days as a fashion editor have I spent so much time thinking about their width and direction. Not since I had it in my power to decree them in, out, or merely in remission for the coming season have stripes been such a preoccupying force in my life.

Lawn-wise, it is my perennial belief they should go lengthways, but my husband is of a widthways mindset. We argue about this a lot, and even when I try and pull rank by trotting out my fashion credentials, it by no means swings the outcome in my favour.

Another source of lawn stress is the enormous pressure we feel to be out there all the time, demonstratively enjoying its fabulousness. To this end, a set of weather-reactive procedures has been unofficially drawn up to extract maximum benefit and value from the garden the minute there is the slightest suggestion of sun.

Once the temperature hits fifteen degrees or thereabouts, the garden furniture comes out and is erected on the lawn, but not before my husband has warned the children that they may only walk on the grass if they are prepared to honour the direction of the stripes and so avoid compromising their flatness and pristine, mathematically correct spacing.

If it reaches 20 degrees, the parasol is very carefully dusted off and slotted into its stand, and there might be tentative talk of patio heaters and barbecues.

It's when the temperature gets to 25 degrees and above that things get really stressful. Mowing and manicuring the lawn into submission has meant that my husband's desire for control has reached fascist-dictator levels of irrationality in the face of any rebel insurgents that threaten his stripes.

In our case, this rebellious insurgency comes in the form of children, ten-foot pink inflatables and a paddling pool the size of Kent. There's making the most of the garden, and then there's making a mess of it. His first instinct was always to scream blue murder, yelling at the kids to get off his precious lawn and go inside and eat crisps and play computer games like normal children.

But, to his credit, he has, over the last two summers, managed to keep a lid on some of his worst stripe-hysteric behaviour. Best not to watch, I tell him, when the plastic water chute is dragged out of the shed and squirted liberally with detergent to ensure a better sliding action.

Best, I suggest, to go inside the house and do what we always used to do during the heat of a city summer – slump on the sofa watching telly in a darkened room, drinking beer. There was no garden then and, therefore, no stress or guilt attached to such delicious indolence. Happy days...

Reason 21: Thatched roofs

During winter, regional news coverage generally majors on villagers-up-in-arms stories about wind turbines, axed youth-club facilities and noisy poultry farms. But in the summer, up-in-arms gives way to up-in-flames, and it's thatch fires all the way.

For three months of the year, barely a week goes by without a handful of television or newspaper items featuring dazed-looking couples standing forlornly in the once-pristine front gardens of their wrecked thatched cottages. Behind them will be the gently smouldering, burnt-out shell of their dream home, next to a few salvaged possessions which always seem to include, weirdly, a standard lamp and a plastic draining-rack (note to all thatch owners: in the event of fire, save the valuable stuff first. Believe me, you'll be needing the cash).

Somewhere off to the side of the picture will be a neighbour with a bucket starting a whip-round, and a handful of not entirely devastated-looking firemen – some of whom will invariably be smiling at the camera – scratching their heads and/or crotches. In the foreground, meanwhile, the newly homeless couple will be detailing their shock, horror and disbelief that such a thing could happen.

But – hello?! – is it really so difficult to believe? It's a bit like building a house out of chocolate and affecting astonishment when the first sunny day reduces it to a molten puddle. Take on a thatch, and it's a bit like tiling your roof with firelighters. You may as well use paraffin-infused paper mitts as oven gloves. I'm not saying the three little pigs got everything right – the red and yellow windowpane-checked trousers they wore in my 1967 Ladybird copy weren't at all flattering – but at least the third of them discovered a thing or two about sensible building materials.

And yet, people are willing to overlook the many downsides of thatched roofs – higher insurance, exorbitant replacement costs – for the pleasure of owning a house topped off with the sine qua non of chocolate-box credentials. Roses round the door – lovely. Leaded windows and a heavy beam presence – great. But, if you are an incorrigible attention seeker and want to be really show-offy about your dream country cottage, you get something with a fringe that looks as if it has been freshly harvested from the heads of several golden-tonsured Texan high-school cheerleaders.

That way, you can be assured a constant stream of envious comments from passers-by. At any given time in the tourist season, there will be a group of at least three out-of-town visitors standing outside, gawping up at your roof, taking photographs and commenting favourably on your impeccable rustic taste. But, for every neatly snipped, diligently barbered thatch, there are 50 more that look an absolute fright – mossy and patchy and betraying the sort of neglect and dishevelment that no amount of one-on-one exclusive client time in the chair with Nicky Clarke could put right.

Let your thatch descend into ragged disrepair and you risk the wrath of the local community, which sets a lot of store by impeccably maintained houses. Personally, I am exceptionally pleased that we didn't have our heads turned by a high-maintenance straw barnet. I know that, in our hands, it would have lost its bristly loveliness pretty soon after we'd taken charge, and the tidy-roof police would have taken their complaints to the very highest level.

By highest level, I mean the chairman of the parish council, which in village terms is like detailing your grievances to the head of the CIA. We have already been shopped for a number of other house-maintenance transgressions, including having the temerity to allow a creeper to do what it was born to do, ie, creep.

A thatch, I fear, would just be inviting trouble, and I don't think we could afford another blot in an already severely blackened copybook.

CAR ON BRICKS

Reason 22: Commuting

There are two scenarios that often precipitate men wanting to move away from the city. The first is catastrophic career burn-out, which finds the high-achieving executive gibbering unintelligibly into his macchiato at his desk one morning, realising he's still wearing his pyjama trousers.

As a result, he resolves to take the wholesale downshifting route. He will sell up and move his family somewhere greener and more civilised, where he intends to spend his days pressing apples, keeping chickens, and building willow structures in the garden.

He will reacquaint himself with the wife and children he has seen little of for the last decade. Punishing work schedules and Blackberry-dependency will be a thing of the past, and he will never again have to tolerate bullying from those macho office bastards with their corporate doublespeak, and their ludicrous daily urging for him to 'get with the programme' and 'sing from the same hymn sheet'. From now on, the only 'extra mile' he'll be walking is over the hill to the pub. The only 'blue-sky thinking' he'll be doing is gazing up at the restful rural cloudscape, wondering where his next gin fizz is coming from.

The other way of moving out of the city is the more popular compromise route. It is where the chief breadwinner is reluctant to surrender his sizeable urban wage packet but craves, for the sake of his children, a better quality of life. So this is how it will work: he will install his wife and kids in an adorable country cottage in a place close to a station and with easy links to town. He will then undertake a daily commute to and from the city, leaving horribly early and returning late, but able to reap the rewards of blissful bucolic weekends, happy in the knowledge that the children are growing up in a clean, safe environment. Besides, the actual travelling part will be nothing but a pleasure, won't it? Isn't commuting from the country into town a much more civilised and rewarding experience than the clammy daily crush of the tube or bus?

The novice rail commuter's optimism is invariably based on images that have remained unrevised since he was sitting on his father's lap, aged five, being read the complete works of Rev

W. Awdry and *The Railway Children*. He thinks travelling by rural train lines is one big, smiley-faced Boy's Own adventure, replete with rolling hills and exhilarating tunnels, all punctuated by immaculately kept stations featuring cheery, benevolent guards with shiny whistles and jaunty caps.

Imagine the pleasure of a commute to work where your first view of the day involves gambolling lambs and boat-filled estuaries. Much nicer than graffiti-obscured grey walls and the depressing back views of row upon row of inner-city housing. There will never be a crush for seats and definitely no pushing, shoving, or early-morning, garlic-breathed expletive-volleying between frustrated passengers. Rural lines run on time and they never have mad, smelly loons propped up asleep in the corner, or dishevelled beggars working the carriages for spare coins. The out-of-town commuter is surely cut from an altogether classier cloth than his urban counterpart. He knows his manners, and never slumps drunkenly in the buffet car stuffing a pasty into his face.

Even his reading matter speaks of superior levels of evolutionary development than those *Nuts*-toting city wideboys. The tweedy rural commuter has a copy of *Which Lawnmower?* open on his lap. His co-travellers are poring over *Total Carp, Caravanning Today* and other titles aimed at the rural hobbyist.

But hang on a minute. This view of commuting is not my

experience at all. The first time I undertook what promised to be a fabulously uneventful and relaxing 70-minute journey into London, the disillusionment began as early as 6.45am, with the race to find a space in a station car park the size of a sandwich (rural train stations are almost always a drive away, not a walk or a cycle ride. This is the countryside remember, where useless establishments such as pig-feed emporiums and rocking-horse repairers are right on the doorstep, but the places you need daily and which are pivotal to the smooth running of normal life are always absolutely miles away).

Not since I holidayed in a villa complex in Spain and had to apply the strategic manoeuvring of an undercover spy to secure poolside sun-bed space, have I experienced so much foul play: drivers ignoring directional traffic arrows; blatant queue-jumping, and cars sneaking into spaces already ear-marked by other commuters. And I thought all those clapped-out cars and window stickers advertising a caring involvement in any number of obscure animal charities signalled nothing but benign rural civility and healthy social responsibility. How wrong I was. This primal, vindictive car-park behaviour was as cut-throat as anything I'd witnessed while living in the city.

More than once, my failure to find a parking space in time has resulted in me missing my train. As far as I can work out, the only failsafe way of being able to park successfully is to arrive at the station the night before and, in the absence of a workable towel-on-sun-lounger option, lay down in a sleeping bag and tough it out until morning.

This is what I have come to, then: someone who spends a great many daylight hours preoccupied with dreaming up car-park space-reserving strategies. I resent this, in ways much more profound than I resent other aspects of rural living. I have been reduced to the status of car-park bore, a stressed and irate station-hater, and I haven't even boarded the train yet.

That's assuming it turns up. The idea that rural lines are run like clockwork by scrupulous, fair-minded country folk who take shiny-eyed satisfaction in seeing their passengers well served, is complete tosh.

It's a well-known fact that anyone who has the temerity to expect to be able to plan their life around a smooth-running timetable is regarded, by rail corporations, with the utmost contempt. But some are singled out for special scorn.

We saps in the sticks are among them. If there are trains to be cancelled, services to be slashed, routes to wipe off the map, then the yokels cop for it every time. This is because train operators genuinely believe that, if you are a catching a train from anywhere more than an hour outside a city, then your motives for travel cannot be anything other than purely recreational.

Standing on the platform, perhaps aimlessly chewing straw

and thinking about nothing more mind-stretching than wind-direction and this weekend's charity barn dance, you can't possibly be trying to get to work.

And even if you are, does it much matter if you turn up or not? Your high-functioning urban colleagues won't miss you. You are a hick, remember, and therefore endlessly dispensable. You are way down at the bottom of the food-chain as far as effectiveness in the workforce is concerned.

If knowing all this doesn't stop you bleating to the train guard about your late-running/non-existent train, then he is sure to have an excuse that will shut you up. The countryside may be lacking in a great many other things, but it never wants for excuses.

Along with the now legendarily lame reports of snow and leaves, out in the country there is extra-thick mist, unpredictable winds and more mud than is strictly natural, and if none of these mess up your travel arrangements, delays can be simply put down to the palpably sluggish pace of things out here, the fug of dazed somnambulance that hangs in the air like an impenetrable blanket.

Another glaring disadvantage of commuting is that, while tube lines may be hellish, cross-city travel is, at least, made up of mainly fleeting visits to hell. A train journey lasting upwards of one-and-a-half hours each way means that the purgatory has to be endured for a far lengthier, more agonising stretch.

There's an unspoken requirement, it seems, that if you're a man and you're on any train after 4.30pm, it is your duty to enrol yourself in the beery brotherhood that converges on the buffet car to drink, swap car-parking tactics and train timetable anecdotes. If I didn't know better, I'd say they were necking all that Special Brew expressly to numb the pain of returning to the countryside from the city, bolstering themselves against the onslaught of green, grinding dullness after another stimulating day in town. Or to steel themselves for another frosty reception from a wife who resents being dumped in the sticks looking after children while her husband gets to live out the best-of-both-worlds part of the relocation deal. As it is, I think they're drinking just because they can.

They will, after all, be collected at the other end. I know this – the whole world knows this – because I have been party to a great many deafeningly loud phone calls home about pick-up arrangements as convoluted and complex as the negotiations to suspend Iran's uranium enrichment programme. Also overheard: wistful goodnights to young children these city workers never see during the week; children whose quality of life was meant to be enhanced by this commuting madness but who, in effect, gained a thatched roof but lost a father.

Reason 23: Working from home

I was easily distracted when I worked from home in London, succumbing to all the usual diversions. Close proximity to a heaving fridge meant that it was just asking to be visited at all times of day. There were invariably urgent tweezering issues that simply couldn't be put off a minute longer. Housework that had languished untouched for months now seemed like the most desirable task on earth, and just the fact that people walked past the house a lot had me running to the window every five minutes.

In any other circumstance, these pedestrians would not be especially interesting, but in the context of delaying a looming deadline, they couldn't have been more riveting if they were three feet tall, dressed in burlesque feathers and had two heads.

In the countryside, then, all this would change. Moving from mid-terrace to a sprawling, many-roomed pile meant I would be able to cut myself off from all extraneous distraction and knuckle down to some serious hard work. My desk would be in a totally silent back bedroom overlooking a view chosen specifically for its tedium: a shed, some climbing ivy, the bins. Nothing going on there, then. Nothing whatsoever to turn the head.

Until I discovered how endlessly captivating it was to observe the comings and goings of a nest of blackbirds shacked up in the eaves. And that silver birch tree off in the middle distance; it was mesmeric the way the light hit its leaves. A family of field mice living in a creeping vine went about their daily life with absorbing audience appeal, and I became a keen observer of scudding cloudscapes and the minutiae of East Anglian metereological shifts. In short, I spent a great deal of time looking out of the window and very little doing any work.

I moved my desk to somewhere less fascinating. It now faced a windowless wall and there would be no excuse for lack of productivity. But the scurrying and scratching of mice behind the skirting boards turned out to be unconducive to hard work. And the blank wall was depressing. There followed a subsequent four changes of room and location as I struggled to find a spot with no distractions.

If self-motivation and the dream of successful home-working is a tricky discipline to nail in the city, it is doubly hard in the countryside. In the early days of our move particularly, living here felt like being on an extended holiday in a rented cottage. In the past, my contact with this sort of extreme concentration of green stuff, wildlife and tranquility had always been connected with rest, relaxation and blissful idleness. It was a set of associations that was more than a little difficult to shake off. The temptation to while away the days loafing around in the garden, drinking gin and tonic on the swing-seat and watching the ducks on the river was impossible to resist. The hardest-working swot alive would find it difficult not to succumb to these seductive forces of indolence. There couldn't have been a richer roll-call of pottering opportunities if you had an annoying floppy fringe and your name was Daniel Radcliffe.

Eventually, with time, application and familiarity (not to mention a pile-up of unpaid bills) the novelty of being in the countryside waned and I forced myself to crack the concentration issue. I settled down next to my Cath Kidston box-files, floral scatter-cushions, coir matting and pencil tidy (such meticulous attention to needlessly elaborate work-station detail is the classic behaviour of the pathological procrastinator) and was a picture of the successful home-worker. But it wasn't long before a sense of gnawing isolation kicked in, a problem that couldn't be solved simply by re-locating my desk or by picking out yet more twee stuff from the Ikea catalogue.

I found that hours, days and sometimes entire weeks could pass without me exchanging more than a couple of words with another adult. And, although I had been freelance while in London and was relatively used to solitariness, at least in a city there was a sense that I didn't have to look far to encounter other people; if I wanted human contact, I simply had to step out of the front door. Crucially, I had a choice. Here, once the children had left for school and my husband for work, the company was almost exclusively four-legged, winged or foliage-based. Aesthetically, no complaints whatsoever. Conversationally, a touch limited.

I started to employ hopelessly transparent stalling tactics whenever anyone rang the doorbell. Is half an hour of needless chat, a tour of the garden and the offer of a third cup of coffee an abnormal amount of time for a householder to want to spend with her wet-fish supplier? And was the bin-man really interested in my holiday photographs, or was he just being polite? When we discovered rats in the loft, a sense of revulsion was quickly replaced by one of keen anticipation. Extermination of vermin required poison. Poison meant pest control. Pest control meant a professional administrator of said poison, which in turn meant a real live human being coming round to the house, climbing up into the roof and, hopefully, staying quite a long time. Only an unhinged, Kathy Bates-type character would contemplate slamming the trap-door shut behind him and keeping this man captive indefinitely. And I hadn't reached that stage yet, surely.

A few pointers, then, for prospective downsizers who doubt their capacity to stay sane in the face of grinding rural isolation. It's important to fight the urge to stay in your nightclothes all day, even if the only company you're expecting is a visit from a wood pigeon. It's wise, too, to glance in a mirror more than once a month. Brush your hair occasionally, but not with the same implement you use for the dog and/or the toilet bowl (an easy mistake to make, granted, but do make the effort). It's probably sensible to get on a train occasionally and visit somewhere livelier and more urban, but only if you have observed all, or at least some, of the above advice. Stay off spirits, at least before mid-morning, and for pity's sake, don't start talking to yourself. It's tempting, because at least you are always assured a reply. But it's also the final, incontrovertible proof that you have turned into an unhinged yokel.

Reason 24: Little men

Is it so much to ask, that in return for generous payment, a little man might be hired to undertake simple DIY chores and gardening tasks? In the city, finding a semi-retired grandad with time on his hands and an easy way with a tool-kit was not only too much to ask, it was downright preposterous. There were plenty of other sorts of men around – white van-driving geezers and Romford wideboys – who would happily botch your boiler repair and tank insulation in exchange for excessive tranches of cash, but decent little men were thin on the ground. All things considered, you stood more chance of securing the services of Madonna as a wet-nurse.

In the country, we told ourselves, it would be very different. little men would be two a penny, gagging for work and, better still, cheap as chips. The village would be heaving with keen all-rounders queuing up to come and sort out our fencing, mend that rusting weathervane and generally keep the garden ship-shape. What is the countryside, after all, but an over-subscribed holding area for these leathery-skinned old boys before they get consigned to the big composting-bin in the sky?

Virtually as soon as we'd put an advertisement in the newsagent's window, the employee of our dreams – a sort of sex-change Mary Poppins with a rake in place of an umbrella – turned up on the doorstep. What were his credentials? He was certainly little, and he was incontrovertibly a man, so that was the first two criteria more than adequately taken care of.

In the aesthetic, show-him-off-to-weekending-Londoners stakes, he looked pleasingly rustic – all ancient cords and the sort of sand-blasted complexion that spoke of a great many long, hard days spent battling the elements while single-handedly constructing stone walls and felling stricken beech trees. Crucially, he appeared skilled enough to take on all the fiddly stuff, while maintaining sufficient levels of diffidence not to parade his competence in a way likely to make my DIY-slexic husband feel like an emasculated loser.

From the hem of his trousers to the top of his flat cap, then, he looked as if he could take on anything, from mending leaky taps to delivering newborn calves to sticking the heels back on those wrecked Manolos.

Looking back, I am trying to remember exactly when and how our cherished little man became that bloody man. Was it when he started complaining about the squalid state of our garden? (He liked, he said, a tidy lawn, and ours was anything but – strewn with toys, ancient dog chews and a jumble of not very attractive garden furniture.)

Or was it when he went AWOL one year during the height of the growing season? (When he finally showed up three months later, he offered no explanation, except to say he'd had 'other business' to attend to. This was the first inkling that he possessed that thing most dreaded by employers of little men, A Life Of His Own. However strongly your primitive instincts tell you to keep such indispensable staff shackled in the coalshed, throwing them leftovers and an old potato sack to sleep on, this sort of behaviour is deemed unacceptable in polite society, more's the pity.)

Or perhaps it was when it became clear that he was getting huge pleasure out of making us feel like incompetent idiots, criticising our choice of carrot variety and heaping scorn on our attempts to prune our own wisteria. And were we mistaken, or were an increasing number of little man's neighbours shooting us hostile, sidelong looks in the village?

It transpired that he was doing the little man version of divulging cleaners' secrets. He had poked around under our metaphorical beds and found the horticultural equivalent of porn mags, dirty pants and mould-crusted coffee cups. The first we knew of his indiscretions was when three people in as many hours commented on our blighted tomato crop. Others tut-tutted about the state of our fence and the overgrown ivy.

But why should we have minded? We were, after all, brittle urbanites. We were thick-skinned and battle-honed. We were practised at repelling muggers, drug-dealers and housebreakers: what were a few moany locals and a shit-stirring gardener?

But somehow, after a few years of living in the incestuous confines of a village, petty gossip about what, in any urban circumstance, would be considered minor detail, starts to get to you. In a small community that prides itself on its neat loveliness, slipping up on house and garden maintenance is seen as the gravest transgression of all. Here, you don't so much present your face to the world, as your house frontage, and if its upkeep is found wanting, you are written off as neglectful, slovenly and more than a little vulgar. You may as well parade round the village wearing PVC and split-crotch pants, advertising cut-price blow-jobs to pensioners every third Wednesday.

It transpired that our little man was stoking up the gossip, while signally failing to properly tackle some of the causes of that gossip. What, for instance, was he doing to correct the exploding climbers, the out-of-hand clematis and overhanging vegetation much maligned by churchgoing neighbours? This was when he broke the news that he didn't 'do ladder-work'.

What did for the little man in the end was that he stopped being endearingly little and got too big. For his boots, I mean. And, ultimately, for his own good. In the beginning, he had certainly proved himself indispensable, with his aptitude for gardening and huge breadth of knowledge about everything from indigenous species of moths and cucumber-frame construction to the best way to eradicate ground elder and force rhubarb. But along with all his undoubted strengths, he had also very effectively demonstrated to us exactly what is signified by the odd in odd-job. He had to go.

We now have another man. He is neither little, nor especially big, but nicely middle-sized. Which seems, on balance, about the right sort of thing to be.

Reason 25: Regional news

If I came from Norwich, I'd keep quiet about it or, at least, I wouldn't feel the need to trumpet the fact on national television. No such reticence for *The Sale of the Century*, a quiz show which ran through the Seventies and whose origin-specific introductory spiel was unique (you didn't, for instance, get *Crossroads* crowing about coming from Birmingham). The arrival on screen of the familiar rotating Anglian silver knight logo preceded the voice of John Benson declaring, to a drum roll and rapturous studio audience applause, 'From Norwich, *The Sale of the Century!*'.

As a child growing up in the Midlands in a strict, parochially minded Catholic household with zero tolerance of anything vaguely effeminate, trashy or foreign (by foreign I mean the area beyond a 50-mile radius of our house), *The Sale of the Century* from Norwich hosted by Nicholas Parsons violated these house rules on all sorts of levels.

Which is why, when I saw the Anglia logo again for the first time in decades soon after we'd moved from London to Suffolk, I felt a surge of latent dread and prejudice. It hadn't hit home quite so starkly before, but now I actually lived in what television, for geographical compartmentalisation purposes, liked to call the Anglia Region. Now, the place my parents had always pilloried as unsavoury by virtue of it being the originator of low-brow quiz shows presented by cravat-wearing pansies (my dad's word, not mine) was 40 miles up the road and categorically not foreign anymore.

Regional news teams reinforced this new feeling of glaring otherness. Gone was the slickly well-groomed cut and thrust of *Newsroom Southeast* and its grave, sharp-edged reports detailing calamitous urban lawlessness on the streets of London. Here was an altogether cosier, plodding, knitwear-heavy set-up, majoring in helicopter sea-rescues and slashed bus timetables.

Before we moved here, I didn't know such things as over-grown hedges and shared right-of-way issues could provoke such extravagant outpourings of bile and heartbreak. As far as I, a recently relocated townie was concerned, the mere existence of hedges and driveways could only be a good thing.

Nevertheless, it transpired that, in the Anglia region at least, hedges, driveways and the laws governing the considerate use thereof got people very worked up indeed.

So, an item involving a hedge, a driveway and, perhaps, a freak weather condition (although it wouldn't have to be very freaky; just slightly out-of-the-ordinary would do fine) constituted a busy, hard-hitting news day. On slow days, an overlong, excruciatingly drawn-out item about a letter failing to reach its destination until eight years after it was posted, featuring lengthy interviews with the postman, the writer, the recipient and the person in the sorting office at Peterborough whose fault it may or may not have been – would be regarded as a good fallback option.

Local news gets the same amount of airtime wherever you live, and the space has to be filled somehow. That's why, when Bury St Edmunds' council proposed the banning of hanging baskets on the grounds they presented a potential head-injury hazard to passing shoppers, it was the sort of idiosyncratically small-town lunacy that was welcomed with open arms by regional news producers.

The furore that resulted when another council launched a campaign to get its occasionally less-than-fragrant bus drivers to use deodorant more regularly also won many long minutes of screen space. An initiative to try and coax house owners to keep eyesore recycling bags hidden away because they compromised a community's sense of civic pride was a long-running story, as was an inter-village sausage-eating competition organised to raise money for a new scout hut. Otherwise, you can almost smell the desperation issuing from the television screen as, under the gossamer-thin guise of newsworthiness and with a lot of recourse to dreadful punning, stories are run detailing how someone's pet cat went missing for three days and turned up 'purr-fectly fit and well' in next door's wheelie bin.

Indeed, the feelgood story, long since jettisoned by national news is a major feature of local East Anglian bulletins. And why wouldn't it be? Out here, there's much to be happy about. We have telegenicity at every turn: we have pretty villages and gorgeous country houses; we have lambs and pigs and Suffolk Punch horses; we have any number of seaside towns and one hell of a lot of weather.

And you know what that means. It means mad-people-swimming-at-this-time-of-year stories. It means bank holiday traffic items, abundant ice-cream-smeared-kid photo opportunities and hottest-day-of-the-year hysteria. It means, in short, that the local news presenters are never at a loss for something to blather on about.

It's when they've got a real hardcore news story that they're in trouble. When barely palatable things do happen in the Anglia region, the newsreaders' homely faces – faces that are well practised at keening over just-hatched chicks and newborn lambs, but complete novices at blood and awfulness – strike you as all wrong. It's like the Oxo mum suddenly spouting profanities over the beef casserole. These are gentle, sheltered, provincial types who simply haven't the depth and range to deliver bad news with the necessary weight.

And besides, wouldn't it help things along if they at least took some grooming tips from the national newsreaders? Regional anchors seem almost bullish in their resolve to ignore even basic laws of televisual presentability. I yell at them a lot, but they are deaf to my advice. 'Get your hair done!' (women). 'Buy a decent suit!' (men). 'Shave, why don't you?' (men and women).

I think the image they are striving to achieve is one of resolutely unthreatening homeliness, and to go too far down the route to slick, prime-time polish would be to alienate those stalwart East Anglians whose idea of looking presentable is to remove their wellies at bedtime.

Clearly, a command has been issued from somewhere high up dictating that the region's female newsreaders should observe the following dress code: 'Ignore all major leaps forward in lipstick trends; stick with glutinous pink from the mid-Seventies. Close your ears to the suggestion that shiny blue eyeshadow went out of favour around the time of the miners' strike. It's not true that seriousness and sleek, grown-up hair go hand in hand. Forget all that stuff about shoulder pads being outdated; they denote authority and will more than compensate for your troublesome blushing problem and inability to pronounce the names of some of the more challengingly titled Iraqi rebel factions.'

And for the men: 'Brash novelty ties chosen for their seasonal relevance are not childish and lacking in gravitas. There is no law against suits that veer very violently to the end of the spectrum categorised as shit-brown. And those squiffy eyes and five o'clock shadow – not at all unpalatable pre-watershed, nor further fuel for non-locals who nurse the creeping suspicion that much of East Anglia is peopled by freakish in-breds.'

(Which, of course, it isn't. If there was even a shred of truth in it, imagine what a news story that would make.)

Reason 26: Flies

If I found flies barely tolerable in London, imagine how hellish it has been since moving to the country. For a good six months of every year, the air is thick with the buggers. And the variety! At least in London, flies had the common decency to limit their species count to three at most, rising to a peak of four or five during the height of summer. A predictable blue-bottle here, a run-of-the-mill mosquito there. And that was it.

In the countryside, there is no such consideration. Here, for a fly, the tempting-stench factor is cranked up to whole new levels of delectability and you barely see the same sort of insect two days in a row. I swear I have witnessed leg and wing permutations that haven't even been discovered or catalogued yet.

And here, we seem to have a lot of mysterious plagues where, for days at a time, you can't move for harvest flies, or ladybirds, or hover flies, prompting excitable reports on regional telly and discussions as to the possible cause. The conclusion is always the same: global warming (let's face it, it's taken the rap for everything. It absorbs blame like J-cloths drink up spilled juice).

In London, I used to hate the clouds of flying ants that would materialise apparently from nowhere on muggy summer days. But now I look back with nostalgia and remember those infestations with something like affection. They were pretty easy to manage. You simply went inside your house and the insects rarely followed you. They weren't interested in interiors; not like country flies, who seem uncommonly keen to set up home with you, even though the rural outdoors is a veritable fly theme-park of attractions – compost heaps to sit on, decomposing rat innards to pick at, roadkill to attend to.

I am convinced there is a lot of premeditated malice where a fly is concerned. Behind the outward appearance of inane, not-very-evolved buzzy thing, lies the brain capacity of a ruthless criminal mastermind. How else do you explain the deviousness and planning involved when flies come into the house during the day and lie low until night falls, waiting for their moment? Then, just as you're closing your eyes, they erupt into life, careering round the bedroom with the sole purpose of ruining your night's sleep.

The obvious question is: why did a pathological creepy-crawly-hater move to the country? What was I thinking? The truth is, I wasn't thinking. We moved during the winter months and so were shielded from some of the countryside's less desirable aspects. Flies slipped through the net, as did stinking fertiliser smells, painfully slow-moving farm vehicles, round-the-clock crop-spraying and other irritants unique to rural summers.

I have worked hard at trying to be more tolerant of a lot of the idiosyncratic out-of-town peculiarities that I used to find incensing when we first moved here. For instance, I can now take on board the hopelessly outdated notion of half-day closing on Wednesdays without wanting to bitch endlessly about the countryside's slack trading. But I don't think I'll ever come round to the idea of flies. I would like to be able to say that we now understand each other, that we have reached a mature agreement along the lines of: if I stay away from you, you must promise to stay away from me. But, despite what I now know to be their enormous intelligence and limitless capacity for advanced neural function, somehow they still don't get it.

Reason 27: Country walks

There is a very small window in a child's life when walking is seen as a fun and novel thing to do. It lasts about six months and comes just after they have learned how to stand, propel themselves forward and trash the house more effectively than when they were simply crawling demolition machines. Very soon thereafter, walking loses its thrill and they demand to be carried, cradled or pushed – anything to avoid making contact with a pavement, road or other hard surface.

But, surely, fields, farm-tracks and foot-paths are an entirely different proposition? Our move to the country, with its wealth of fascinating, nature-based sideshows, would usher in a whole new era of enthusiasm for open-air perambulatory activity. No more sit-down protests in the middle of inner-city zebra crossings. No more screaming fits and shoe-throwing episodes while walking – and I use the term loosely – down a busy high street in full view of every nicely behaved, shoe-respecting child in the neighbourhood.

It became clear soon after our move that, although the backdrop may have changed, the attitude hadn't: the children intended to keep up exactly the same level of go-slow campaigning and noisy protestation – just with much quieter surroundings in which to express their shrill displeasure.

It didn't take long to find out that sitting down in a farmyard is a far smellier and dirtier procedure than sitting down outside Sainsbury's. Hurling a shoe skywards in the country is riskier than jettisoning it in town. The chances of it landing in something sloppy and unspeakable-smelling are high. The possibility of it getting lost in the undergrowth and/or being carried off into the woods by hungry animals is very real. You'd think this knowledge alone would prompt better behaviour but, instead, it just seemed to intensify their worst townie traits. They screamed blue murder at the unfamiliar sight of placidly grazing sheep, erupted into hysterics at the merest suggestion of mud on their wellingtons and circled cowpats as if they were unexploded landmines. Not the enriching family strolls we had in mind, then.

We tried different tactics. We learned to avoid provocative, inflammatory words such as fresh air and exercise. Instead, we drew heavily on the adventure and exploration angle. After all, it worked for the Famous Five; take away the ginger beer and weird Uncle Quentin and what were they doing but simply messing about outdoors ie, going for a walk?

As our children grew older, gruntier and even more reluctant, we put an inordinate amount of effort into selling the idea properly. It wasn't uncommon for a strategy meeting to start on a Friday evening ahead of a projected walk two days later. On no account would we tell them that we were going out on foot to promote good health and wellbeing; we would market it, rather, as an incentive-driven, goal-oriented proposition – sometimes with sums of money involved. Then we would work like stink at following through with lavish promises of limitless muddy puddles, big sticks, endless processions of fascinating agricultural vehicles and, God willing, an assortment of bloodied, mangled and gut-spewing field-dwelling creatures.

If none of the above enticements had them scrambling into their anoraks, we would throw in the promise of a bag of crisps and a lemonade at a pub along the way. Once they had left point A with point B in mind (point Bs are important to children: without a point B there is, literally, no point), the walks were often successful. But never so successful that we wouldn't have to market them twice as hard all over again next time round.

Five years on, the arguments have stopped and the screaming fits ceased. Our walks are calm, orderly and, dare I say it, enjoyable. This isn't anything to do with the children having come round to our way of thinking; it's because now they refuse point blank to join us and, in any case, are old enough to stay at home watching telly and engage in other screen-based, brain-meltingly moronic activities with no cardio-vascular merit whatsoever.

It's not at all what we'd had in mind when we moved to the country, but then, what is? We are, by now, well used to having our dreams rubbished, our whimsical ideas chewed up and spat out, and our airy-fairy notions about healthy lifestyle choices ripped apart and left for dead. Much like the impressively mauled, rank-smelling muntjac we came across while out walking the other day. The children would have been thrilled.

Reason 28: Driving

Round here, you can set your clock by the ladder-man. Every morning and every evening, at 8.15am and 5.30pm respectively, he makes exactly the same journey through our village. He travels to and from a market town ten miles away in his beaten-up red Peugeot 305, three ladders of differing sizes lashed inexpertly to the roof-rack.

On the positive side, his unwavering regularity performs a valuable service. A neighbour who lives on the high street knows she is likely to be late for work if she has not left her house by the time the ladder man rattles past her window each morning. In the subsequent few minutes, she logs the following responses: first gratitude at the jolt to her memory provided by the ladder man, then panic at her lateness, followed quickly by abject despair when she realises she will be stuck behind him all the way to the station.

And stuck behind the ladder man is a place no sane person would want to be.

This is because there is no circumstance in which he would ever contemplate exceeding 27.5 miles an hour. Not if he was being chased by a slavering herd of wildebeest (unlikely round here, but for drama's sake, stay with me). Not if he had been stabbed through the heart by a flying wooden stake (it could happen) and his life depended on swift arrival at a hospital. And most certainly not if his vision is uninterrupted and there is mile upon mile of safe, straight, open road ahead of him. If anything, this only makes him go slower. On a short journey, being stuck behind the ladder man might be just bearable – amusing, even – but for a distance of ten miles, with a train to catch at the other end, it provokes the sort of homicidal rage you don't really want to be entertaining first thing in the morning, at the start of a working day.

I have been in a long queue of cars trailing him several times, and found myself incensed on several levels. First, he seems completely unaware of the fist-shaking, gesticulating, profanity-yelling snake of irate drivers behind him, threatening to bludgeon him to death with the blunt end of one of his own paintbrushes. Second, if he made the fundamental improvement of attaching his ladders more securely, he might be less worried about speeding up a bit. Third, what is he actually up to? More than once, it has occurred to me that there is no decorating job, no building work at the other end of his journey. No; he is simply taking to the roads at the busiest time of day to deliberately slow people down and spread stress where there ought to be mellow, bucolic bliss.

And that's the other thing about the ladder man: he serves as an irritatingly insistent reminder that I am still a long, long way from achieving the sort of easy-going, slow-paced, time-flexible attitude that should surely come with living in the country. Why rush? Why not take a deep breath, drive slowly, look out of the window and embrace the beauty of my surroundings?

So what if I'm stuck behind a belching farm vehicle doing five miles an hour while emitting a light spray of manure all over my windscreen? And shouldn't I be enjoying the novelty of following a gargantuan combine harvester eight miles down winding roads, sneezing violently from its straw fall-out? What's not to like about a herd of cattle blocking the road and lowing lazily as they make their somnambulant way from one field to another, accompanied by a farmer who looks like he last washed sometime during the late-Seventies?

The point is, all this may be a novelty once or twice, or for weekending visitors looking for some authentic country road action, but if you live here and have things to do, places to go, children to get to school and appointments to keep, it makes you want to slash your wrists with the nearest rusting farm implement.

I estimate that my capacity for violent road rage has more than quadrupled since moving to the country. City dwellers moan about slow-moving traffic and horrendous bottlenecks, but I would say that, on balance, not going anywhere because you haven't got a choice is slightly less irritating than going slowly on a quiet open road when you really ought to have options, if only that ponderous octogenarian in the M-reg Metro would speed up a bit.

You can't overtake the old fools because the roads swoop, bend and dip like fairground rides. Not that this stops some people. The prevailing belief is that quiet little country thoroughfares are safer, but actually people drive like lunatics on rural roads because they assume that, while the visibility is often atrocious, there are, nevertheless, miles of deserted road around those corners and bends, when in fact they are often covered in ice, floodwater, an endless procession of suicidal wild animals and, when you're least expecting it, one of those M-reg dodderers.

To drive carefully is also to maintain standards of showy politeness, and this has taken some getting used to. In London, I barged and bullied, swerved and swore my way round town along with everyone else. Here, on the other hand, a simple three-mile journey might entail six waves, fourteen extravagantly mouthed thank-yous and countless cheery smiles as you are let through on roads the width of pipe-cleaners. For neighbouring villagers always expect acknowledgment when you drive past them. To ignore this basic rule of small-community etiquette is to invite untold hostility. They know where you live. They know your number plate. They will freeze you out for months to come.

Driving in the country, then, means maintaining a constant, unremitting, high-frequency state of red-alert for acts of extravagant decency that might be required of you. That means no pleasant day-dreaming or harmless introspection while behind the wheel. No zoning-out to the soporific tones of *You And Yours* on Radio 4.

Since moving to the country, I estimate that I spend a good 50 per cent of my waking hours thinking about driving, talking about driving, or actually in the driving seat. This is because out in the sticks we spend more time in our cars than we do in our houses. After breathing, driving is the life skill you most require in order to function effectively. Virtually everywhere you want to be is a car journey away, especially where children are concerned. Living in the country with even modestly popular teenagers means kissing goodbye to boozy weekend evenings; adult enjoyment dwindles in direct proportion to your children's burgeoning social lives, as you find that you are forced to stay sober and alert on Saturday night in order to complete a 50-mile journey at 11pm to collect a gaggle of screeching teenagers from some far-flung nightclub, then make a wildly circuitous route home down a set of labyrinthine backroads to dispatch them all back to their various villages – a round trip that could take going on three hours in total.

All this, of course, makes a complete mockery of moving to the country to live a more wholesome, cleaner lifestyle when, in fact, since relocating, your carbon emissions have rocketed and petrol consumption gone through the roof. Mention this to what you hope are your environmentally aware children, on the way back from yet another late-night party in a neighbouring county, and, chances are, they will not immediately promise to look into bus timetables or lift-sharing with friends. No; they will pull a horrible face and scream at you about how unfair it is, and what an apology for a parent you are, topped off with the knife-to-the-heart comment all reluctantly rural teenagers come out with eventually: 'I hate you! I didn't ask to come and live out here in the middle of bloody nowhere!'

To which there is really no sensible answer other than to shut up, keep your sorry, selfish head down and keep driving.

Reason 29: Gravel

There is plenty of girly, rustic stuff with which to lure women to the country – rambling creepers round the door, pulse-quickening thatches, free rein to cover every available surface in heartbreakingly pretty florals – but what would swing it for an averagely red-blooded man? Even if he remains resolutely unmoved by everything else the country has to offer, he is sure to feel stirrings towards at least a couple of rural attractions. A ride-on mower is one. A luxuriant gravel driveway is another.

Any man who says he is not seduced by the sound of car tyres scrunching their way languorously around a sweeping arc towards the front door of a country pile is either a liar or a homosexual.

What is so appealing about gravel? Like so many things in life – nut brittle, Bath Olivers, a crisp Granny Smith – it's the crunch that does it.

But it has to be the right sort of crunch. When I first set eyes on the huge expanse of gravel driveway that came with our house, it never occurred to me that the sound that would issue from it would be anything less than the sensually distinctive one I had heard on any number of television period dramas and news footage of the Profumo affair at Cliveden.

But we were in for a disappointment. The sound our gravel made was more like the unimpressive crackle that might result if you applied a thin-soled slipper to a puddle of soggy Rice Krispies. What we had expected was definitely more akin to something very heavy falling from a great height on to a generous consignment of cornflakes (that's proper, robust Kellogg's cornflakes, and not flimsy, own-brand pretenders).

To say my husband was upset would be an understatement. He hid in the shed for half an hour, and he doesn't like sheds.

We sought advice from a red-blooded friend nearby. He applied a hob-nail boot to our patchy, thinning driveway and agreed that, yes, the crunch was less a crunch than a wet fart and would need some work to bring it up to cornflake standards. We would have to buy more gravel. A lot more gravel.

Now, I had never thought of gravel as something you could actually buy. Didn't it just exist, like air and sky? Apparently not. To accumulate gravel in the volumes we required would involve one of two things. We could either collect it ourselves by the pocketful from the beach at, say, Felixstowe, a process that, given the size of our driveway, would take roughly the same amount of time it takes to build a modest Olympic village. Or we could make the short five-minute trip to the building suppliers down the road.

We duly made our way to what I can confidently describe as the most unappealing retail outlet I have ever visited. (And, yes, this is taking into account the fact that I have set foot inside Lidl and at least one branch of Morrisons.) Very obviously conceived by men for men, the notion of seductive point-of-sale display had clearly never troubled these gruff blokes in overalls. Everything was simply heaped haphazardly in piles in a yard. You had to know what exactly you were looking for before you went in. Nothing about the way this stock was displayed was geared towards must-have impulse buying. I doubt very much that anyone has ever wandered in and bought six meters of 4x2 simply because of the irresistible way it was stacked against a wall.

Anyway, we queued up to talk gravel with one of the yard men, knowing we were soon going to be exposed as lamentable DIY know-nothings. How, for instance, is gravel measured? Bags? Lorryloads? Tins?

When we eventually put in our meek request for 'some' gravel, we were directed outside and told to choose which grade we wanted. I opened my mouth to discuss the only kind of grading we knew about – cornflake quality as opposed to Rice Krispie – but thought better of it. From the way he was thwacking a metal tape measure impatiently against his thigh, it was clear he was keen to get back to his proper, knowledge-able customers, the ones who knew the correct vocabulary for discussing such materials as 30mm copper-piping and high-density tank insulation.

We waited until no-one intimidating in many-pocketed painter's overalls was around, then chose our gravel based on the sound it made when a foot was applied to the various different piles we'd made on the ground. This took quite some time and I wished we had taken along a selection of different shoes, not to mention both cars, to measure the gravel's success on our stringent crunchometer.

Two enormous bags of gravel were subsequently delivered to our house, which, over the next few days, I distributed over the existing moss-blighted expanse. After many hours of back-breaking work, I stood back to reflect on my achievement.

But admiration soon turned to frustration. I had no issue with the gravel's new, vastly improved textural depth; it exceeded all my cornflakey expectations and, even after a downpour, crunched marvellously underfoot. But I hadn't reckoned on weeds pushing through. Weeds were not part of the Cliveden-crunch equation, and I was furious.

A weed-knowledgeable neighbour directed me to remedies with idiot-proof literal names such as PathClear. But this noxious stuff doesn't annihilate them, it just turns green weeds brown. In subsequent weeks, I spent rather more time than I care to recall on my knees, scrabbling around on the ground, cursing and yanking them out manually.

Except the dandelions, which don't respond to yanking or, indeed, any sort of force applied with ordinary garden tools. Never be fooled by the sort of insistent Bill and Ben propaganda which presents weeds as polite, docile things with smiley faces. They are, in fact, mean-minded antichrists intent on ruining your life.

Other bad things about gravel: it gets kicked on to the lawn and buggers up the inner workings of the mower; it gets stuck in the treads of shoes and finds its way into the house – it subsequently marks, scratches and ultimately ruins your expensive slate floor tiles; the dog eats it and, more often than not, requires veterinary treatment as a result; it requires regular raking in order to maintain even coverage; children complain bitterly about it because it's rubbish for bike-riding/ballgames/skateboarding and almost any other outdoor activity they are interested in, bar the popular, and now prohibited, sport of gravel-wrestling.

I'd say we fell out of love with gravel – seductive crunch or no seductive crunch – pretty soon after we moved in. Even after all that hard work and effort to attain the desired Kellogg's sound effect, gravel has proved itself to be a confounded nuisance to live with. Lately, we have been looking to replace it with low-maintenance paving. Just as soon as I get my courage up, I intend to go down to the building supplies yard and discuss it with the scary ruler-thwacking man. If he asks what kind of paving I am looking for, I am tempted, this time, to use a more businesslike descriptive aid, instead of the now rather crass-seeming cereal analogy.

I shall tell him, with all the technical flair I can muster, that we are leaning very much towards a smooth, urban, Rich Tea finish as opposed to the rougher and more rustic HobNob.

Reason 30: Squirrels

Since moving to the country, I have been careful to ensure that there is always, at any given time, a ready supply of the following items on the table by the back door: assorted low-denomination foreign coins, a selection of discarded Christmas cracker novelties, various stones of different shapes and sizes, and, on the floor underneath, a pile of old shoes.

A more storage-conscious person might regard this jumble of domestic trash as symptomatic of the worst kind of sloppy housekeeping, but not me. Miniature tool kits, plastic whistles, de-commissioned French francs; this isn't rubbish, it's valuable weaponry.

No one likes a war, least of all one that is waged across the peacefully undulating expanse of an idyllic country garden, but l find myself a reluctant participant in the ugliest stand-off I have encountered since we moved here.

There is, it transpires, disputed territory at stake, and that territory comes in the form of a heavily fortified, imposing structure hewn from solid wood and standing some six feet off the ground. For the sake of simplicity, let's call it a bird table. The first time I saw the squirrel brazenly pilfering nuts, I reacted as any ordinary country-dwelling bird-lover would; I shouted at it and it ran away. When it returned less than five minutes later, I tried psyching it out with a long, murderous stare followed by a stern talking-to – relayed in a chilling monotone – littered with squirrel-related expletives.

It was during its third audacious raid that I made the difficult decision to deploy heavy artillery. When several large handfuls of gravel scooped from the path and delivered by sustained aerial bombardment failed to spook it, I turned to the coins. From my position of attack just inside the back door, deutschmarks and pesetas rained down on the animal, followed by a few hundred Italian lire. To no effect. Such was the cocksure arrogance of this twisted creature, it seemed entirely possible that it thought that, by throwing money, I was somehow showing my appreciation. No doubt it says quite a lot that it was only when some muscular US currency was introduced that the squirrel looked, for the first time, genuinely terrified.

Not so terrified, however, that it has been deterred from its dogged campaign of provocation, encountering, at each visit, an ever more deranged and banshee-like opponent. Now, a great many waking hours are spent staking out the garden from my vantage point in the kitchen. The area around the bird-table looks like someone has disgorged the contents of an especially tacky amusement arcade machine onto it, and I find myself eaten up with resentment, brimful of loathing for my bushy-tailed tormentor.

I am sure I speak for many people when I say that you don't experience real hate until you move to the countryside. I nursed grievances in the city, but nothing like this. This squirrel-induced grudge has depth. It has texture and nuance. It has all the slow-burn, energy-release potential of a gigantic wholegrain loaf.

The day I cold-bloodedly slaughtered a mole with a pitch-fork was the day I felt I had become halfway integrated into the cantankerous ways of country folk. No more amateurish retaliation using old bottles of nail varnish and toy cars hurled with some force from upstairs windows.

I see now that the reason country dwellers get so worked up about the issue of using what the government vaguely describes as 'reasonable force' against intruders is because they've cut their teeth on four-legged pests and know all too well the distress unwanted intrusion can cause. They also know the kind of homicidal rage that kicks in when moles are churning up your beloved lawn and pesky squirrels are after your nuts. As a newly ruthless defender of my property – but, as yet, without the air-rifle I am so longing to own – I challenge anyone to come and have a go if they think they're hard enough, but a word of warning: to the arms cache by the back door I have now added a mallet, a potato masher and an extremely intimidating-looking shoehorn.

Reason 31: Garden machinery

Give a man the choice between test-driving a Ferrari or being let loose on anything from the extensive John Deere range of garden machinery and he'd almost certainly choose the latter. Great, big, over-sized tractory things in shiny primary colours speak to the latent Tonka toy-fancying toddler in all men. They masquerade as essential lawn-maintenance products, but only a fool thinks they're anything other than great big man-toys. Operating a lump of metal this huge and brash is one of the few remaining lost pleasures of boyhood that can be indulged in public without risk of the driver being branded a pervert, a freak or a Mummy's boy.

Ride-on mowers are the last word in covetable garden machinery, and appeal to the impulse in men that would have liked to have acquired an HGV licence and be able to do risky stunts involving ramps and long rows of buses, if only marriage, children and sensible SUVs with imaginative stowage solutions hadn't got in the way.

Because they're doing it in their own back gardens, ride-on mowers give men carte blanche to drive round like lunatics in mad crazy circles and still not alert the suspicions of the police or cause fatalities – give or take a defenceless woodland creature or two. If they close their eyes – and they often do – they might almost imagine they're engaged in extreme quad-biking on the dunes of the Kalahari, as opposed to tidying up a modest patch of lawn in the home counties. When we moved to the country, the discovery of a garage full of grass-trimming accessories was greeted with unbridled elation by my husband, and resulted in a marked change, for six months of every year, in his normally docile personality.

During winter, when the only thing that grew in the garden was our distaste for its stark, twiggy barrenness, he would remain totally uninterested in all outdoor tasks. But come spring, at the first sign that the lawn might possibly be coaxed into looking like something other than a football-desecrated Somme, he metamorphosed from a mild-mannered layabout refusenik into a gear-slamming petrol-head.

Suffice it to say, summer evenings weren't the lazy, tranquil, Sauvignon-steeped affairs I had envisaged. Instead, come dusk,

186

the garden would erupt to the sound of sputtering machinery and clouds of noxious emissions as my husband mowed as if his life depended on it.

But there's mowing and there's relentless scalping. If Knowing When To Stop is a difficult lesson for men to learn in all sorts of areas, where grass cutting is concerned, it's virtually impossible.

I don't think my husband realised he had a problem until, one summer night at around 10pm, he had been mowing for four straight hours and was now churning up clods of earth where grass used to be, swigging from a bottle of Budweiser and laughing maniacally. It does not give me any pleasure to report that eventually, he had to be forcibly removed from the ride-on and led gently up to bed. By way of compensation for having his beloved tractor taken away, I tucked him up with a hot drink. If he'd asked me, at that point, to read him a few of the less challenging chapters of my son's old copy of *Bob the Builder and the Big Yellow Digger*, I might well have consented.

After that sobering moment, which ended with ignition key-confiscation and a padlock on the garage door, he took up the slightly more genteel art of strimming instead (he had his eye on the chainsaw, but that was vetoed). As it turned out, strimming revealed itself to be no less seductive in terms of its potential for imaginative fantasy role-play possibilities. I happened to glance out of the window during one Sunday of wildly irresponsible privet-butchery, when it was clear he wasn't just a bloke with a whirring blade and a protective mask. No; he had cast himself as Darth Vader wielding a lightsabre and contemplating a life of domination on the dark side.

And just watch the enthusiasm evaporate the minute something goes wrong. After the relentless hammering it had been subjected to at the hands of a newly anointed grass-cutting addict, it wasn't that surprising when the strimmer sputtered a few times then packed up. Nothing about my husband's previous townie existence had prepared him for repairing malfunctioning power tools and the appeal of garden machinery began to fade almost as quickly as it had taken hold.

It was after a particularly upsetting frog-mashing incident with the ride-on that any residual interest in machinery finally drained away. Now a gardener does the grass. Within the hours of daylight, and with the proviso that he locks the shed behind him. Just in case.

Reason 32: Bonfires

In the countryside, there is always something vile that needs comprehensively torching – diseased farm animals, expired household pets, rat-ravaged carpet offcuts pulled from the shed, Alan Titchmarsh's entire back catalogue – and it's a good job too, otherwise bonfires might not exist, and without bonfires, life in the countryside might not be worth living.

In the early days of moving here, after a long and stressful day pretending to know what I was doing in the garden, the process of setting light to a huge, roaring bonfire was valuable therapy. It was the polar opposite of nurturing and coaxing and gently tending. It was destructive, violent and final. It was nothing to do with giving life, and everything to do with snatching it away. It spoke to the nasty, aggressive, slash-and-burn terminator in me and, if I am being honest, gave me much more of a thrill than dividing snowdrop clumps or planting out seedlings. But I know I am not the first urban exile to embrace this nihilistic pyromaniacal pleasure.

In the city, where are the opportunities for a little recreational fire-starting? Piddling little barbecues in your poky backyard, that's where. Failing that, arson, which seems an extreme way of getting your kicks. Better, cheaper and easier on your criminal record to move to the country and burn things with impunity.

Consider the allure of the bonfire: it's the closest you are allowed to get to violence and public affray without being arrested. Under the guise of Tidying Up The Garden, it offers an outlet for some of the pent-up anger and resentment associated with rural life that would only end up being target-ed elsewhere – at all those smug experts whose advice has signally failed to work when applied with my inexpert grasp of gardening. During some of my angriest moments, my fantasy pyre has included Monty Don, Bob Flowerdew and Charlie Dimmock (if only for the marvellous kindling opportunities offered by all that mad hair).

Even so, it soon became clear that I was approaching the business of bonfires with rather too much townie enthusiasm, and not enough sensitivity to my immediate surroundings. There is, it seems, a set of unwritten rules about bonfire etiquette that I fail to observe.

The first inkling that I was being rather too free with the matchbook came from a neighbour who revealed herself to be acutely hedgehog-sensitive. She told me that bonfires are barbaric and needless, and that underneath all that garden debris lie nests of squalling baby animals that need protection, not red-hot firelighters applied to their nether regions.

Then, one bank holiday weekend, another villager offered his thoughts on my voracious bonfire habit. He arrived at the front door looking a touch irate, with bits of ash in his hair and smut on his face. Hadn't I thought to establish the wind direction before setting light to six months' accumulation of leaf litter and old bookshelves? Of course I hadn't. Nor had I checked the weather forecast. If I had done so, I might have found out that the sun was due to come out, thereby rendering me a horribly thoughtless killjoy for smoking out the entire village on a rare, fine spring day.

In London, fire and smoke rarely attract suspicion, much less disapproval. When we lived in Hackney, our house and all its contents could have burned down in full view of the entire street, and raised barely a passing glance. Here, however, village dwellers' nostrils are primed – like German Shepherds nosing the luggage carousel at Bogota airport – to pick up the merest hint of a suspect smell. They will claim that this permanent state of olfactory red-alert is because they have beams to protect, timber frames to safeguard, thatches to preserve, clean country air to maintain.

They call it conscientious neighbourliness. I call it putting the dampers on a perfectly innocent pleasure. They have ruined my fun.

In the end, it was all the complaints, as well as the accidental burning-down of an apple tree and an unfortunately located Spacehopper that eventually curbed my hunger for fire. These days, I make increasingly frequent trips to the municipal dump. However, hurling bin-bags full of garden waste into a big skip isn't nearly as satisfying as torching stuff. More than once, it has crossed my mind that what this huge accumulation of dry waste is crying out for is a carefully aimed match, just to liven things up a bit.

Reason 33: Weekending friends

It's not the most inexpensive way of securing lasting friendships – reading groups are vastly cheaper, as are evening classes in basket-weaving – but it's certainly effective. Anyone who has serious doubts about their personal popularity rating should consider swapping their city house for a place in the country and then watch while, overnight, they become the most irresistible companion anyone could wish for.

When our friends – and, in some cases, only distant acquaintances – first heard about our move to the countryside, they lost no time divvying up weekends as if our house was a timeshare in which they owned a major part. But we didn't mind; we were more than happy to welcome all comers. On the one hand, we were terrified of being lonely once we'd relocated to the arse-end of nowhere. On the other, in the first few months of our move, we felt an overwhelming need to gloat and brag about our preposterously gorgeous new country house and garden.

Friday night became designated gloating night. In preparation for the arrival of weekending visitors, we would spend time perfecting a look of carefully dishevelled bucolic bliss – bare feet, loose linen clothes, casually strewn floorcushions – then, ice bucket filled and gin bottle poised, wait for the sound of tyres on gravel.

As our visitors' car came to a standstill, we would rush out to meet them with the urgency of A&E staff hurrying to pull critically injured accident victims from ambulances. Which, in the circumstances, isn't such a crass parallel. These were damaged, pained-looking people, stressed and dazed from a long day at work in the city, followed by a brutalising brush with M25 rush-hour traffic, and they were in urgent need of sanctuary.

In retrospect, they were probably quite keen to sit down, relax and enjoy a drink and do little else for the rest of the evening, but we invariably had a packed agenda of showing off to get through, and the 'full tour' of the house would be offered – or rather, insisted upon – shortly after their arrival.

God, we were pleased with ourselves. Smug doesn't even begin to cover the way we felt when we flung open the door of yet another gloriously beamed bedroom, pointed out a fabulously characterful inglenook, or showed them round the vast garden with its orchards and lawns and ducks gliding lazily up and down the river.

All for the same price, we pointed out emphatically, as that pathetic London terrace with miniscule town garden we'd left behind!

They nodded and cooed appreciatively. Some of them talked vaguely of making a similar lifestyle change in the not-too-distant future, but declined to name even an approximate date. Later, in private, we would pour scorn on their cowardly indecisiveness. We had, we concluded, been a lot braver than most. We hadn't just done what disconsolate city dwellers normally do and indulge endlessly in dinner-party chat about swapping town for countryside with no intention of carrying it through; we had done it. We had made the move, and we felt nothing less than heroic. In our view, this wasn't just a fairly undramatic relocation 80 miles out of London; this was something akin to how intrepid pioneers must have felt venturing on horseback into the hitherto undiscovered, parched plains of the Wild West.

If it was hard work looking after another family for a week-end – is eight too high a number of dishwasher-reloadings to undertake during a single day? – it seemed a small price to pay for being told repeatedly how shrewd and admirable our move had been. We were lucky, we were brave, they said. We had adapted to the welly-wearing ways of rural folk, embracing nature, gardening and the whole shabby-chic lifestyle as if we were born to it.

But as time went on, we became less and less enthusiastic about the prospect of visits from city friends. For a start, if we were spending virtually every weekend entertaining, when was all the DIY and gardening going to get done? When were we going to visit local farm-shops, attend fêtes and quiz nights and generally integrate with the locals?

Secondly, it was exhausting. After a particularly gruelling run of five consecutive weekends playing host to visitors, we were wiped out, and needed to confront some hard truths. The original idea was that these thoughtful friends would come generously armed with provisions and their own bed-linen. They would more than pull their weight, and willingly undertake their share of the cooking and clearing up.

What they wouldn't do was turn up earlier than planned with dogs and extra visitors we weren't expecting, and without wellies or waterproofs or any of the other elementary basics of rural protective wear. Nor would they insist on staying up till the small hours drinking all our booze, expect a rolling breakfast buffet service the next morning, use all the hot water, or slope off to the nearest pub while the finishing touches were added to their Sunday lunch.

There were a few who habitually arrived full of enthusiasm for the latest idiotic food fad to hit London. There would be loud, previously unannounced declarations that they had given up dairy, or wheat, or both. They weren't doing red meat, or fish, or, indeed 'anything with a face', and only organic sprouting grains would do. My heaving fridgeful of delicious local produce bought at some expense from the farm-shop was swiftly reclassified by guests as a no-go area of toxic banned substances.

I recall that the words parasitic, pretentious freeloaders were habitually uttered during scandalised late-night de-briefing sessions between me and my husband. What did they think they were playing at? With a few exceptions, visiting friends would not lift a finger all weekend. They would pitch up fully expecting a well-deserved relaxing break away from their hectic city lives, and where better to get it? At the home of their newly idle country friends. Never mind that we were employed too; the fact that we worked from home, in near-perfect surroundings, meant that it couldn't possibly be considered real graft. What we now represented was a free weekend away, with all services, meals and entertainment thrown in.

And, as if this wasn't enough, some of our old friends seemed to think their sole function as weekend guests was to bring some smart cosmopolitan chat and urbane repartee to the lives of their slow-witted newly rural friends.

Quite often, their remarks would carry a snide edge. They mocked our quaintly backward village pubs (rubbish food, crap beer, no ice) and the funny-looking locals, and predicted a time in the not-too-distant future when we would be talking with broad Suffolk accents and indulging in a little light in-breeding.

Eventually, we discovered that a tough rural winter is nature's way of seeing off overly keen weekenders. We noticed a sharp drop-off when the nights drew in and the promise of balmy summer bliss had waned.

It turned out to be the wake-up call we needed. The sense of isolation and abandonment brought on by winter was a sure sign that we needed to stop being so reliant on our old friends for company, and get out and make some new, local ones.

Now there is some sort of balance. Visits from city friends are not weekly, but occasional occurances that fit around our new circle of village friends. Often the two groups mingle and, much to the surprise of some of our townie visitors, it's not the wildly mismatched stand-off between backward yokel and slick urbanite they might have feared. One London friend, prior to a visit, expressed his concern that he knew naff-all about DEFRA, the hunting bill or crop-rotation, and what the hell would they talk about? In the event, they discussed the same mixed bag of things all middle-aged parents talk about:

house prices, schools, Broadband technology and male-pattern baldness. They found they had more in common than they first thought, including the fact that, by the end of the evening, they were both as reluctant as each other to help empty and re-load the dishwasher.

Reasons not to move back to the city

I could move back any time, I bullishly reply when people ask what an incorrigible complainer like me is doing, occupying prime green real estate that could be better enjoyed by a genuine country-lover; someone who could properly exploit the garden's vegetable-growing potential, and not let an entire patch of perfectly serviceable rhubarb languish unharvested for four years on the trot.

I tell them I would return to the city tomorrow, if only the children weren't at last putting on such a good show of having settled in here, and if only those neighbours – always smiling, despite the relentlessly isolated, silent surroundings – would stop turning up with Prosecco of a summer's evening, wanting to sit in our vast garden on the willow-shaded bridge overlooking the river and the ducks and voles lazily patrolling the banks.

Yes, I could give it all up in a heartbeat, and move back to the Smoke and be my real self again – the impatient, grabby, intolerant individual who knew and loved London as a privileged insider, who owned it, ate it up, and, I am keen to stress, is still a long way from spitting it out again.

So it is with some reluctance that I have to report a certain crumbling of resolve. Latterly, visits to London have not been the thrilling re-acquaintance with urban zip and hum they once were. I get off the train at Liverpool Street and it's not the old me standing there, street-smart antennae twitching and alert; it's a cowering, utterly provincial hick wincing at the racket and wondering how long before I can rejoin the train for the journey home.

On the rare occasions I venture across two zones (the equivalent, in yokel terms, of a trans-Siberian hike), I find myself even more flummoxed. These days I look at London's busier areas with the simmering disapproval of a parish councillor eyeing up a lacklustre market square and finding its floral displays wanting.

My sense of communal pride has gone through the roof and no-one is more surprised than me. Walking round the city, I find myself imagining what the village magazine would have to say about streets thick with buskers, beggars and dead-beats.

I find myself wanting to pick up litter, straighten people's collars, buff doorknobs, file a detailed report to the county council about the disturbing rise in noise pollution or, at the very least, start a rota for scrubbing down the bus shelters.

Streets lined with lights and shop fronts used to thrill and delight; now I find their insistent garishness overwhelming. In the country, my world – particularly my retail world – has narrowed so profoundly that any sort of choice or decision-making has become baffling and stressful.

It's only when I'm safely on the train home, rubbing up against the sports jacketry and absorbing the comforting – yes, comforting – whiff of egg and cress that it occurs to me that lack of choice isn't necessarily a deprivation, it's strangely liberating. And perhaps I am not significantly diminished as a person just because I don't, anymore, get a pulse-quickening rush to the head when I descend the escalator to the Underground.

But to confess all this, I feel, would be to admit that my wellies have sunk rather deeper into country mud than I am entirely happy about.

I could move back to the city any time, remember.

I'm A Teacher
Get Me Out of Here!
Francis Gilbert
1-904977-02-2 PAPERBACK £6.99

At last, here it is. The book that tells you the unvarnished truth about teaching. By turns hilarious, sobering, and downright horrifying, *I'm a Teacher, Get me Out of Here* contains the sort of information that you won't find in any school prospectus, government advert, or Hollywood film.

In this astonishing memoir, Francis Gilbert candidly describes the remarkable way in which he was trained to be a teacher, his terrifying first lesson and his even more frightening experiences in his first job at Truss comprehensive, one of the worst schools in the country.

Follow Gilbert on his rollercoaster journey through the world that is the English education system; encounter thuggish and charming children, terrible and brilliant teachers; learn about the sinister effects of school inspectors and the teacher's disease of 'controloholism'. Spy on what really goes on behind the closed doors of inner-city schools.

"Gilbert is a natural storyteller. I read this in one jaw-dropping gulp."
Tim Brighouse, Commissioner for London Schools, *TES*

The Cruel Mother
A Family Ghost Laid to Rest
Siân Busby
1-904095-06-5   £7.99

In 1919 Siân Busby's great-grandmother, Beth, gave birth to triplets. One of the babies died at birth and eleven days later Beth drowned the surviving twins in a bath of cold water. She was sentenced to an indefinite term of imprisonment at Broadmoor.

The murder and the deep sense of shame it generated obviously affected Beth, her husband and their surviving children to an extraordinary degree, but it also resounded through the lives of her grandchildren and great-grandchildren.

In Siân's case, ill-suppressed knowledge of the event manifested itself in recurring nightmares and contributed towards a prolonged bout of post-natal depression. After the birth of her second son, she decided to investigate the story once and for all and lay to rest the ghosts which have haunted the family for 80 years...

"A gripping tale of madness and infanticide during the Great War... Powerful and disturbing"
Margaret Forster

How to be a Bad Birdwatcher
To the greater glory of life
Simon Barnes
1-904977-05-7   £7.99

Look out of the window.
See a bird.
Enjoy it.
Congratulations. You are now a bad birdwatcher.

Anyone who has ever gazed up at the sky or stared out of the window knows something about birds. In this funny, inspiring, eye-opening book, Simon Barnes paints a riveting picture of how birdwatching has framed his life and can help us all to a better understanding of our place on this planet.

How to be a bad birdwatcher shows why birdwatching is not the preserve of twitchers, but one of the simplest, cheapest and most rewarding pastimes around.

"A delightful ode to the wild world outside
the kitchen window"
Daily Telegraph